I Am... Everything I'm Not

Kelly Klemetsrud

Edited by
R.S. Regester

Editor in Chief
Sabra Klemetsrud

authorHOUSE®

AuthorHouse™
1663 Liberty Drive
Bloomington, IN 47403
www.authorhouse.com
Phone: 1-800-839-8640

First published by AuthorHouse 7/1/2010

ISBN: 978-1-4490-9565-9 (e)
ISBN: 978-1-4490-8727-2 (sc)

Library of Congress Control Number: 2010901877

Printed in the United States of America
Bloomington, Indiana

This book is printed on acid-free paper.

With a special thanks to
My wife Sabra,
My daughters Bridgette, Kelleigh-Jaymes, and Kasi,
Dr. Mark McKenzie,
Olga Friauf & Lisa Nutt
For your influence and input upon this book.

On Dec.6, 2009 I was on my way to Buds, (The best sports bar to watch a game in Chattanooga) from Cleveland, to watch the Dolphins play the Patsies and on the way my chest started hurting me. I stopped and got a cold drink to cool what I thought was a bad case of heart burn. The pain was like a burning, vise type grip upon me and I got no relief from my cold drink. I decided to stop at a grocery store to pick up some Prilosec, because I wasn't going to let some heartburn stop me from watching my Dolphins take it to Brady & Co. I popped one in my mouth and waited a few minutes and nothing. The burning, vise type grip was still there. So I decided to wimp out and go back home and let my wife take care of me.

That burning, vise type grip was getting hotter and tighter. I was starting to get scared now as I activated my emergency flashers. I was traveling just under 80 m.p.h. with my flashers on as I was motioning for cars to get out of the pass lane so I could go through. Some drivers were a little dense and I had to flash my brights at them repeatedly for them to move over.

My thinking was, if I stopped and pulled over for help, I would have to wait for the police to get there and then the ambulance. I could be dead by that time. So I forged ahead hoping I could just get to Skyridge Medical Center in Cleveland. Just 10 miles to go. The burning, vise type grip was not letting up, as a cold sweat started to come out on my face, neck and chest, making me very clammy.

I pulled up to the hospital, leaving my car running at the emergency drop off, and staggered to the front desk where I told the lady I was having severe chest pains. Hoping they would take me more seriously than that poor slob up in Philadelphia a few weeks ago, I crumpled down on a seat, hugging a coffee table, as I started to cry like never before. The pain was outrageous. I waited under a minute in the waiting room. Then they wheeled me into the ER. These guys were ultra professionals. Stupid me, I kept apologizing for being there, again and again.

After they gave me some morphine for the pain, the burning, vise grip in my chest did ease up. They did a battery of tests on me and my pain had eased. I was hoping that this just wasn't heartburn. The nurse asked me, "Wouldn't you want this to be just heartburn instead of a heart attack?" I said, "Yes, but how bad would a heart attack hurt then if I had one of those?

After about an hour to an hour and half, I was asking for something to stop the pain again. I was hoping I wasn't sounding like some kind of addict. They gave me an EKG and it showed I was having a heart attack, right then and there, at Skyridge Hospital. I was sobbing and crying and apologizing over and over, because this stuff doesn't happen to me, especially at 47.

They again took charge and stabilized my condition. They told me I was going to take a helicopter ride to Memorial Hospital in Chattanooga. I thought, cool, my own personal Trauma show.

Sometime before I got on the helicopter, I red lined. I was dead. No bright lights. No white robes or a choir singing. No elevator to Heaven or Hell. St. Pete was no where to be seen. Nothing but blackness. Then I heard the air-tech asking me if I was with them. I said, "Yes, do I need to say it louder?" They had brought me back using the defibrillator on me twice. I'm a big guy, 6'4' and weigh about 285 lbs. I was thinking that there was no way my big butt would fit on the little stick to put me into the copter. But fit I did, and believe me, there is no room in those copters, at all.

Off we went into the darkening night sky. Those two air-techs, that were with me, did their best to keep me alive. Not sure what they did, but it worked. Then as we descended onto the heli-pad, the pilot zigged when he should have zagged. I showered those techs with what was ever left over from breakfast, but they never complained. They told me to stop apologizing and said that most people usually lose it at that time.

I was rushed into cardiac-cath, where two arteries were found blocked. They put a stint into the big artery and put me on bloodthinners, for the smaller artery that was blocked. I was shipped off to cardiac ICU, where I was given the best care possible night and day for two days before being put into a regular room. The third day I was sent home.

I wish there was some way I could reward all the people who helped save my life, parked my car, and never blinked as I vomited upon them (3 different times), defecated in front of them and then cleaned me up. But, I'm not that rich. These people do this everyday, and it's not pretty. And for a paycheck that's probably no bigger than yours or mine. These people are Angels, put here to help the fallen, to help the dying, and if possible to bring them back from the dead.

All in all, 1/3 of my heart was damaged. I need to take my blood sugar (was in the 350's) and cholesterol (was at 892) more seriously and I need to lose weight, smartly by eating smarter. It won't be easy. I've been fat for almost a decade. But through counseling and hard work I won't replay this past Sunday.

My heart pumps now at 40%, instead of the regular 60%. I'll be a prime candidate for congestive heart failure if I don't get into better shape.

I was given the same kind of service, at both hospitals, that a President or a visiting Head of State would have received. And, I cannot thank all the techs, nurses, and doctors enough, for saving my life. To these people, it's all in a days work but to me they are all heroes. They are all Supermen and Wonder Women, at least when they are at work.

Thank you, thank you, thank you, thank you God for saving me from certain death, yet again. I seem to have survivors remorse. I mean, over $100,000 was spent on me, to keep me alive. Why was I saved? How can I repay God for saving me yet again?

I guess the answer is, you can't. You can't repay any of the heroes that saved your life, just like you can't pay God back for all the miracles he gives you each day. All you can do is to live your life to the fullest. And in doing so, you will be repaying everyone back, who had a hand in saving your life.

Endless Thanks,

Kelly Klemetsrud

I dedicate this book to my beautiful wife, Sabra. I told her the other day, I'm glad she hasn't divorced me, because then I'd have to get skinny. I enjoy being fat and happy with my wife and children. Without her, I wouldn't be who I am today. With her, I am all the good things I possibly can be. Without her, I'd be that player that puts himself before all others. Thank God I get to grow old with you, Sabra.

Thanks,

I love you.

Table of Contents

Foreword

Hi everybody,

Welcome to my second book. This book is just a tad late, meaning I had to kill more of my darlings. But, that just means more love went into the final product. My first book, 500 Ultimate Truths, is still out there waiting for you to buy it. This book is all original and I hope you enjoy reading it as much as I did writing it. I do hope to ensnare you with my words so you actually become part of the poem. You will see passion in my poems and I hope you can feel the passion as well. You will see things from my point of view and optimistically can get a better understanding of the many different aspects of life around you. Hopefully this will broaden your horizons, as it has mine.

These are great poems and you should enjoy them. Are they the 101 best poems ever written? That's for you to decide. You can tell me all about it by dropping me an e-mail, myultimatetruths@aol.com. I will answer all who drop me a line.

Go Dolphins!

Go Orioles!

Smiles,

Kelly Klemetsrud

I Am... Everything I'm Not

This book is about all the things that I'm not, and in doing so, is really an inside look at all the things that I am. As a child, I hated poetry. I thought it was too girly for guys to read. Going through my divorce from my first marriage, and the legal fight I had just to see my children; I found that poetry is very passionate and very therapeutic. I found the passion that I had been missing in my first marriage, by writing it into my poems.

I'm not talented enough to write my poetry in rhymes, but each one will strike a cord to the reader on a personal or maybe even a spiritual level.

The poems are listed in alphabetical order, after we start with the first poem I ever wrote and two others that narcissistically describe the author (sly smile). I believe I am the best karate teacher there is, but there was a time, when I was a pretty accomplished fighter. In 1989 I was in a bad car accident and I was told I could never fight again. This was a hard time for me with my rehabilitation, an impending divorce, not being able to see my children, and trying my hardest to prove that I could continue to function as well as I did before my accident. Even though that was a losing battle I could not admit to for years to come. My first poem is entitled "I Am... in the Squared Circle", and I swear I remember that poem from almost twenty some odd years ago as if I had just dreamt it. It was the most life like dream I have ever had. I have updated it somewhat from the original text.

I hope you guys enjoy my poems. I have always felt that I could write a poem about anything. If you think of a subject you would like to see me write about, drop me a line, and see if I pull it off. I would love to read your thoughts about my poems. I'm a needy bastard and I crave your reaction to my prose. Your critique will help me become a better writer. Please be on the look out for my next book, Perceptions of a Father. Until then, thank you and enjoy these poems.

I Am...

...in the squared circle,
Yet again for the first time.
And just like the last time I was within it,
The squared circle cries once more.
It's been over twenty years since I was taken from my element.
Twenty years since that car accident that ended my fighting career.
Twenty years since I gave up not only my dream,
But the best life anyone would ever want to live.
You can't imagine the thrill of being in that squared circle.
You can't imagine how much I miss the action.
We've all heard it before ...
The thrill of victory and the agony of defeat.
To bask in the substantial rewards that come with a victory,
Or to wallow in the unholy depths of your despair,
When you realize that your best was just not good enough.
But I had this dream one night that sent me back in time.
I found myself back in the squared circle.
Uniform was on as well as my fighting pads.
The bell rang and I was deep in the action.
Fists as well as feet were flying fast and hard.
Sweat was rolling down my face.
The taste of my blood energized me as I got hit.
I set my opponent up for the knockout.
Sidekick to the stomach and then backfist to the head,
Finishing him off with a nice ridgehand to the face.
Even in my dream I knew this was but a dream,
But I refused to let reality rear its ugly head.
This time was different because this time it was for real.
By some miracle I had become whole once again,
From Elephant man back to being Superman.
I woke up and immediately shouted to my Mom and Dad.
I wanted to share this miracle with them.
But alas! it was not to be.
Reality did rear its ugly head,
My disability was still with me and,
Not only did the squared circle cry at my loss,
But I did as well.

I Am...

...me.
Welcome to my world.
Guess what?
You are me as well,
And just to make it extremely confusing,
I am not you, though.
Seems like we have a paradox of identities here.
Ha!
Look at it this way:
You are entering my world,
When you read one of my poems.
And in so doing,
You will soon become of my world.
I on the other hand,
Don't have a clue about you,
Or your world.
Are you escaping your world when you visit mine?
Is my world a refuge for you,
Or some type of ungodly punishment?
Punishment for what?
Only you know the answer.
I can only imagine where you are from,
And what your world is like,
Or how similar both our worlds are.
When you enter my reality,
You will live in my world,
For as long as you read about it.
In living in my world,
You will experience the thrill of the best victories,
Or the agony of the worst defeats.
We will become the most intimate of lovers,
Or the most despicable of villains to each other.
I hope visiting my world,
Will have a positive impact upon your world.
Even if what you read
Turns your reality upside down.
These poems are a collection of my wanderings
Over the faceted kaleidoscope of my mindset.
What do you want to take from my world?
Are you some rogue pirate,
That plunders and pillages,
Wherever you may roam?

If so,
You will love my poems.
Because each poem has an unlimited supply of booty to be harvested,
To be used at your own discretion.
Are you reading my poems
To learn from the mistakes of another?
If so,
You will learn
That I have made a lot of mistakes in my life.
Some of the mistakes were so fun,
I had to make them quite a few times over.
You might say I have a list of my favorite mistakes,
Because I revisit them so often.
Hopefully,
Once you see the pattern in which I live,
You will adapt to your own pattern,
So you won't make my mistakes.
If you do make my mistakes,
I guarantee you,
That the results will be the same for you,
As they were for me.
So read on, McDuff!
A grand adventure awaits you,
That starts deep in the recesses of your mind.

I Am...

...the World's Smartest Man.
That is my blessing,
That is my curse.
If no one believes that you are the World's Smartest Man,
Does it really matter if you are?
I've unlocked some of the greatest mysteries
That have vexed mankind for eons.
I've discovered the Tower of Babel
Hiding in plain sight,
(The Great Wall of China),
I've explained how tornadoes work,
(They run on electro magnetic currents).
I've told you the true origin of global warming,
(it's happening from the inside out, instead of the outside in)
By depleting the Earth of its protective layers of oil,
To shield us from the heat of our inner core.
I've explained how a planet the size of Earth,
Couldn't have a moon the size of ours,
(The moon was really a symbiotic sister planet to our Earth).
I've solved the mystery of 666 in the Bible,
Where we should stop looking for a physical number upon a person,
But a person who is this number,
Like the 666th World Leader,
(That's who your Anti-Christ will be).
And what kind of response do I get when I exclaim my findings?
Do people marvel at my brilliance?
Do they wonder what next ancient riddle I will solve?
Alas,
They don't.
They just laugh at me,
And discount everything that I believe is true, as mere rhetoric.
They give me the same old company line for all of my findings.
The Chinese built the 2,200 mile wall to keep,
Marauding barbarians from invading their country.
If there were that many barbarians invading China at that time,
This wall would have never been built.
But these learned people will believe their falsehood,
Instead of the truth I have presented.
They tell me tornadoes just happen when bad weather
occurs and are unpredictable and follow no set path.
Then why does a tornado never occur,

Where the foundations are dug deep,
Interfering with the electro magnetic fields of the storm?
This is why tornadoes don't occur in downtowns or at football stadiums.
They tell me that the global warming we are experiencing,
Is just a natural cycle of things.
The inner core is not expanding as we deplete the Earth,
Of its natural protective barrier against that heat.
They say that the moon was expunged from the earth,
In a violent collision with a comet.
And lastly,
The Bible says 666,
So we should look for the actual number 666,
Upon the forehead of this person.
Instead of thinking that this number upon the forehead,
Is the mantle of leadership,
And should look for the person who is the number,
Instead of the number on a person.
And "they" say my theories are too hard to believe?
Where do people come up with this crap,
That is taken for gospel?
But that's the price of being the smartest person in the world.
No one will believe you.
My blessing is that I can solve these mysteries,
My curse is that no one will believe me.

I Am...

...a black man.
I am not an African American.
I don't know what it means to be an African American,
Because I am a Black American and I have been one all my life.
Do you know what being a black man means?
Does it mean that I look different from you?
Or do I talk differently than you?
Does it mean
I'm more likely to be a criminal than you are?
Only shallow people think these things.
Society as a whole
Is 12% criminal,
Why is it then that my people are so singled out?
I really have no idea why am I so stereotyped.
What have I done to you?
I pass you on the street and if you are in your car,
You make sure I hear you lock your door.
Some people have asked me,
Why don't I go back to where I came from?
How can I do that?
America is where I came from.
I have as much validity to claim Africa as my home,
As you claim France or Sweden to be yours.
Africa is a land comprised of many foreign nations.
Why would I call that home?
I can't speak or understand the language,
I wouldn't eat the food nor could I read the newspaper,
Or watch the television over there.
So what if my great, great, great, great, great grandparents,
Were brought over here in chains by the Portuguese?
Considering the options they had,
It was probably the best choice possible.
Just like it was the best choice possible,
For everyone else's ancestors who made the trek to America.
I'm sure most everyone else's ancestors had a choice,
Which would be the difference between my ancestors and yours.
But look at the choices my ancestors had to choose from.
Die as a free person or live as a slave,
And hope for redemption and freedom?
As long as there is life there will always be hope,
So what choice did my ancestors really have?
Would your ancestors have made a different choice

If they were in my ancestors shoes?
If time heals all wounds then I guess it's all a moot point now.
But guess what people?
All the chains are gone now,
And I refuse to be shackled down by the constraints of the past.
Isn't America the land of the free?
I will not be considered 3/5's of a man,
Like those who went before me had to endure.
Would you?
My blood is just as red as anyone else's.
My country expects me to spill it when they call,
To defend our freedoms,
Mine and everyone else's,
As well as our collective way of thinking.
Why is it I'm looked upon with such scorn,
For dating a white woman or marrying a white woman?
In years past I could've been put to death just for love.
People today still look unfavorably towards it.
Why would anyone be concerned if I date a white woman?
Are they afraid I'll turn her black?
If I love a white woman,
Have I betrayed my race?
Not hardly, because love is truly colorblind.
As long as my woman and I care about each other,
Love each other and support each other,
Believe and love in the same God,
It matters very little if we are of a different color.
We are the same on the inside.
What we look like on the outside is of little importance.
I am a black man and I haven't had it any rougher or easier
Than I have made it for myself.
If I succeed or fail,
It will be through the grace of God,
Not by the hatred of ignorant, selfish, petty, people.

I Am...

...a butterfly.
You know,
The diva of the insect world.
You know there is a poster of me,
In every larva, pupa, and grubs bedroom.
But fame is such a fragile thing,
Much like me.
I might come from very humble beginnings,
But once I burst out of my cocoon,
Like a phoenix reborn,
BOOM baby!
Pop art with wings,
Bringing a splash of color wherever I go.
We all know that silence
Is the ultimate weapon of power,
And a picture says a thousand words.
I might flutter,
Without an utter,
But I know I can be seen,
Both loud and clear,
No matter how much noise is about me.
If I were human,
I'd be Andy Warhol,
And just like with Andy,
There is nothing dull or dreary about me.
If you want dull and dreary,
You must want a moth,
And I ain't no moth, baby!
So the next time
You stop to smell the roses,
See if you can catch me being a mural in motion.
Fame might be a fragile and fleeting thing,
Very much like me,
But then so is life,
Both yours and mine.

I Am...

...a cat owner.
That means I am also a servant.
I am a servant to my cat.
In ancient Egypt,
Cats were revered as gods.
My cat still has this mindset.
My cat expects to be worshipped at all times,
And keep food and water at Her Highness's disposal.
But Her Highness,
Is still the Queen of the Urban Jungle.
I bought two massive,
Mean looking,
They-can-smell-your-fear,
Doberman Rottweilers.
I got my boys to guard my house,
I thought I would have some fun,
And have my boys meet Her Highness.
They eyed each other:
It was a Mexican standoff.
My boys were starting to get anxious,
But, Her Highness just kept her cool, licking her paw.
They couldn't understand why Her Highness showed no fear.
My boys growled,
And Her Highness continued to lick her paw.
Then it happened,
In a blink of the eye.
Her Highness took a step,
And my boys got ready to pounce.
Ready to show they were in control.
Her Highness hissed at them with a long loud hiss,
And my boys pounced twenty feet,
Backwards.
The law had been laid.
Her Highness is still Queen of the Urban Jungle,
And we are but her lowly subjects,
To pet and stroke her,
Whenever and wherever she desires.

I Am...

...a Child's Valentine's Day Card.
And I'm usually
The first taste of love
That every child experiences,
Outside of their family.
Whether I'm written
In pencil, pen, or crayon,
I always say the same thing,
Accept me.
Accept me for taking the chance of liking you.
Liking you or loving you,
It's really all the same to me.
Because I have set myself up
For love,
Or public humiliation.
So the choice is yours,
My very first Valentine.
Accept me for me,
Or accept me for liking you.
I'm taking one small step for childkind,
One giant leap,
Into the abyss of love.
You can knock me or
You can make fun of me.
Some might consider me brave,
While some might say I'm stupid.
But you can't say
I don't have great taste.
Happy Valentines Day!

I Am...

...a clown,
Ha, ha, ha, ha,
Life is one big gas,
Ho, ho, ho, ho.
There is a method to my madness,
I assure you.
I'm hoping that you will be soooooooooo busy
Laughing with me,
Or laughing at me,
You won't notice my tears.
And let me tell you,
Those aren't tears of joy either.
You see,
Comedy is the most serious form of tragedy there is.
It's a fact,
That the funnier one is,
The more tragic their life has been.
Pity the poor fool,
Who has lived a tragic life,
And is not the least bit funny.
Now that's tragic.
I'd rather hear your laughter,
Than feel your pity or scorn.
They say that laughter is the best medicine and if that's true,
Through my feeble attempts to make you laugh,
I can heal what is hurting,
If not in you,
Then at least
What is hurting me.
Have you heard this one before?
There are these two potatoes standing on a street corner.
One of these potatoes is a prostitute.
I guess she thinks she is a hot potato.
But how can you tell the regular potato from the prostitute potato?

The prostitute potato is wearing a sticker that says IDAHO..!!!!

I love that joke.

11

I Am...

...a demon,
And I only exist in your mind.
And yet you fear me
As though I were a living being.
I come in a variety of shapes and sizes.
I can be anything-
From your wildest dream,
To your worst nightmare.
And if I'm in a really naughty mood,
I can be both at the same time.
We demons are without number.
Do you know where demons come from?
Most people would say Hell,
And this is the correct answer.
But most people don't know what or where Hell is.
People always make jokes that Hell,
Is their work,
Or at their home with the mate and kids,
Or Hell is visiting their in-laws,
Or. . .
Well, you fill in the blank.
I was not born in some
Infernal, fiery, dank, nether region of Hell.
Take my appearance for example.
I don't look like most people would picture a demon to look like.
There are no horns on the top of my head,
Or a tail coming out of my. . .
As for my origin,
You know it better than anybody,
Because you created me.
Does that piece of information surprise you?
Do you think God created demons?
Silly, silly, reader.
When man fell from Grace,
Man also got the ability to create demons.
God creates angels out of living beings,
No matter how wicked or evil an individual might become,
Every person has a greater capacity,
To do more good than to do evil.
Man makes his own demons,
Sometimes out of inanimate objects, such as
A "demon" in a bottle,

That uses a tall smooth frothy glass to get to you.
A bag of "demon" dust,
With its fine white powder,
Will make you think you've been to Heaven
As you sink lower into the depths of Hell.
Being a speed "demon"
Might be fun and exciting,
But the danger that it poses,
To you and others is just too great.
How many of my brethren are in your life right now
As you read this poem?
Can you recognize the demons now in your life?
Are you a slave to your computer?
If so, you have made your computer a "demon" unto you.
Do you find that you have to have certain things,
Such as a cigarette,
Or a stiff drink,
Or a quick snort,
To get through the day,
Or to finish your appointed task?
Anything that has that much control over you,
But only comes to life
On your say so
Is a demon!
What about people that have control over you?
Do you have a taskmaster of a boss,
Or a very domineering mate?
Are they not demonic?
Now pay attention.
They are not demonic personally,
Only their influence over you is.
Stop letting people or things control your life.
Stop being your own worst enemy,
And start taking control of your life.
The choice is yours.
Stop the madness
Of making the wrong mistakes so often.
Or, find out what Hell is all about
If your demons go unchecked.

I Am...

...a doormat.
I must be one because I have so many people walking on me.
I thought I was a stepping stone,
But when they stop and grind their heels into you,
You realize you are a doormat.
I didn't start out being a doormat.
I used to be a lover,
Parent,
Employee,
A valid citizen of the community.
And above all,
I used to like me.
But no more.
My lover has no respect for me.
No matter what I bring home,
It never measures up.
So now I'm looking for my next ex-lover.
My children have no respect for me,
I'm just the one who clothes and feeds them,
And waits on them hand and foot,
Putting all my wants and desires last on the list.
They want me to be their friend,
Instead of being a loving and concerned parent.
You can't be a good parent if you do this.
My boss takes me for granted,
Because I show up for work each day.
A vacation would be nice,
But I can't afford to take the time off.
Just like my boss can't afford for me to go on vacation.
My neighbors used to wave and say hi to me,
Now I seem to bother them by saying hello.
I used to think I could conquer the world.
Now I'm happy if I can conquer a night's sleep,
Which all too often is by myself.
How did it all slip away?
I guess I just told you how it all slipped away.
And if this sounds all too familiar,

You are a doormat as well.

I Am...

...a habitual sinner.
Sometimes it seems,
I can't sin enough.
Is there ever a time we don't sin in our daily lives?
In the old days it was always,
Actions spoke louder than words.
Jesus upped the ante on us though.
If things weren't hard enough for us in the first place,
Jesus went and told us,
Thinking about a certain sin was as good as doing the sin.
AAAAARRRRRGGGGGGHHHHHHH.!!!!
Does this mean,
That we now sin in our dreams?
How can we control what we dream about?
Or would this be considered something like manslaughter,
As opposed to first-degree murder?
That is just one end of the spectrum.
On the other end is the daily drudgery of living.
I have been taught since infancy to do the right thing.
Why do I sin every day then?
I know the difference between right and wrong,
And there is no gray area.
It's either right,
Or it's wrong.
I got enough spankings from mom to realize this difference.
I have never committed a crime towards my fellow human,
But if we are to believe Jesus,
I've committed genocide against a culture I do not like.
I've stolen from the rich,
And kept it for myself.
I've had sex with more women than King Solomon had wives.
I've senselessly adulterated, murdered, and stolen,
From anyone that had something I wanted.
I probably even blasphemed God,
With my thoughts of ruling the world in my own image.
I wake up lusting after women who aren't in my bed,
And never will be,
If they have a say in the matter.
I plan intricate robberies and thefts,
Of things that I would never use if I owned them.
I never act out my "plans".
I'm a sinner,

15

Not a criminal.
There is a difference between the two.
You can be a sinner without being a criminal,
Just like you can be a criminal without being a sinner.
This is where humanity blurs the concept
Of our own mortality,
And immortality.
Supposedly,
God punishes sinners, right?
Why do we think God will punish a criminal then?
And why does
Man, be it male or female, punish criminals,
But supersedes his authority
By trying to punish sinners?
Is that not a sin and a crime rolled up into one?
Why am I such a habitual criminal?
Probably for the same reason,
I am a habitual sinner.
Because I choose to do all things evil,
With my own free will.

Just like you do.

I Am...

...a homosexual.
It's amazing how that one word can alter the mood.
We fought against Hitler in World War II,
And his ideas of how one race is superior.
Yet I am considered to be less of a man,
Because of my sexual preference.
Homosexuals are easily the most persecuted people on earth.
Add to that the fact,
That a homosexual might be,
Black or Jewish,
And it just adds fuel to the fire,
Of racial and sexual intolerance.
Homosexuality has been around since almost the dawn of time.
Every nation,
Culture,
And religion has homosexuals.
Homosexuals are also the most feared as well.
Why are we feared?
With that fear comes hatred and ridicule.
I've been called it all,
From gaywad,
Faggot,
Princess,
To commie pinko fag.
Are people afraid that we will turn their Fathers,
Husbands,
Or even themselves gay?
It doesn't work that way.
Homosexuality is not a disease.
You can go to the store and catch a cold,
But you can't go to the store and become a homosexual.
We are not born homosexuals.
There is no gene that we are born with
That makes us gay.
Wouldn't that make us homosexual by divine intervention then?
If God did not want me to be gay,
I wouldn't have been born with this certain gene.
So since I was born with this certain gene,
God must have wanted me to be gay?
That would make it waaaay too easy then.
No,
We are homosexual by choice.

17

Just like the choice to do drugs or not,
Or to smoke,
Or to drink alcohol.
Nobody forces us to make these choices.
And nobody forced me to become gay.
I just chose it,
And I'm comfortable with my decision.
That is the way it should be.
There is nobody to blame Johnny for being Gay,
Except for Johnny.
Will we go to hell for being homosexual?
Will heterosexuals go to hell for being straight?
These right winged fanatics who quote the Bible are lunatics.
If homosexuality is such a serious "crime",
Why don't the Ten Commandments
Say, "Thou shall not be gay"?
Sodom and Gomorrah were not destroyed
Because of homosexuals.
They were destroyed because of immorality.
Jesus Christ never said one word
About the "evils" of being homosexual.
Paul wrote letters about how being gay was wrong.
But let's get serious,
That was some serious homophobia going on with him.
The bottom line is this:
I know I am God's favorite child,
Just like you are.
If you have a problem with me or someone else being gay,
That's exactly what it is.
Your problem.
Deal with it.
If you can't,
Pray about it and let God help you with it.
He's just waiting on you to ask for help.
Worry about your own salvation,
Not mine.

Mine is already taken care of.

I Am...

...a loser.
This is the one paper
That I never wanted to write.
It's the one paper
I tried to make myself believe
I was not qualified to write.
But let's man up,
I'm the most qualified on this subject.
No time for a pity party.
I've been at the pinnacle of success.
I've gone through Hell and back to obtain my glory.
I've risen from the ashes in victory,
Only to be knocked back down
Into the depths of despair.
I've had to pick myself
Up off the floor,
Just to get knocked down again.
There is a fine line between being a winner,
And being a loser.
A kicker that misses a winning field goal
By three inches is a loser,
But if he makes it by three inches,
He's a winner.
Either way,
He has to be a talented player
To be out there in the first place.
Just because you lost,
Doesn't mean you have to act like a loser.
Losing teaches you something winning can't,
And that's humility.
Being a loser means
You didn't give up.
You manned up,
And lost.
Whether at sports,
Scholastically,
Love,
Or anything you made an effort at.
You just came out on the short end of the stick.
But at least you had a chance,
No matter how small it might have been.
The end result might have been different.

You aspired to scale The Heights of Olympus,
But with Gravity being such a harsh mistress,
You came crashing down to reality.
But at least you had a chance.
Never lose sight of that.
That is why you play the game,
And at least you did get to play.
That's better than not playing at all.
You had a chance
To rewrite history,
And to become a legend
Of your own making.
Everything in life,
Counts as a win or a loss.
So losing amounts to experience,
And experience amounts to wisdom.
But in reality,
The only way you can be a true loser
Is if you give up,
Give up and don't care.
If you don't learn anything from your losing experience,
Then you really did lose.
And that's a shame,
Because
It's not whether you win or lose,
Until you lose.

I Am...

...a machine:
A being without any feelings.
At least,
My employers would like to think so.
I'm supposed eat, drink, and sleep, my work.
I work in the medical field,
I am a pharmacist.
My employers are very gracious
To give me a whole thirty minute lunch break each day.
Then get this absurdity,
I have to make up the lost work time of my lunch breaks,
By working Saturdays for NO PAY!
When was the last time my employers sacrificed their lunch,
Or worked for NO PAY,
Or even worked any weekend?
My employers are very concerned
About not being able to find enough competent employees.
But if they just treated everybody
The way they treat themselves,
This would be one well oiled machine.
I thought I was hired as a paid professional,
Not somebody that does slave work.
Am I not protected by some kind of law?
Are OSHA or labor regulations
For everybody else but my field of expertise?
I know I graduated at the top of my class.
I even have a doctorate in pharmacy.
Since I'm on salary and not paid hourly,
My employer takes full advantage of this.
I can't leave until the job is done
At this pharmaceutical sweatshop.
My boss leaves at 4:30 pm on the dot everyday.
That means even though we are understaffed,
New hires come in the morning and leave at lunch,
Never to return again.
I might have to work 12 to 14 hours a day,
With no overtime being paid.
My employers don't mind paying almost double the salary
For a temp,
Because they can take that salary off
As a business expense on the company's taxes.
Why don't they just bring in more help

21

To get the job done?
I thought sweatshops were things of the past,
Or
In some 3rd world country.
But guess again people.
Sweatshops exist here in America.
A lot of people depend on me to do my job right.
My job is one of those life and death jobs,
If I make the wrong decision,
Someone could die.
Would you want that somebody to be you?
Does my employer care if someone I care for dies?
Only if they could be held liable.
Other than that,
They want everybody to hang on by a thread.
That's how my employers make their money.
By profiting off other people's misery.
I know one word that would get my bosses attention,
One word I could evoke,
(UNIONIZE)
That would get me fired on the spot.
Funny,
I think my it's employers that are the real machines here.

From a very disgruntled employee.

I Am...

...a minister,
Which is very different from being a preacher.
Jesus Christ himself commissioned me to be a minister.
Just like he did to you and everybody else.
Supposedly,
Preachers are called to preach.
Called by whom I wonder?
I didn't hear anything.
And I know that God speaks for the world to listen,
Not just to a select few.
(Sorry Pat Robertson)
I minister to the masses,
Through my words, actions, and my convictions.
It's true,
That my words and actions fall terribly short at times,
But my convictions are steadfast.
They never waiver or are swayed to go with the crowd.
Like the man that is supposedly the head of the household,
A preacher is the spiritual head of a church.
A minister is the spiritual head unto himself or herself.
There is an old adage,
That Satan goes to church each weekend.
And while it's sad but true,
Satan is usually behind the pulpit every Sunday.
Am I saying all preachers are morally repugnant?
Heavens no!
That's like saying all topless dancers are whores,
And we know that's not true.
And Jimmy Swaggart can testify to this fact.
A minister ministers,
Trying to alleviate the pain and suffering,
That goes with everyday life.
Ministers console more than teach.
Churches today have become giant tax-free conglomerates.
They are more interested in keeping it in the black,
Than saving someone's soul.
That means a preacher is just a CEO,
Or a puppet whose strings are pulled by "the elders".
You see,
There's more to being a preacher,
Than just a humble minister.

I Am...

...a moment,
And it happens in a split second,
That lasts a lifetime.
Where both parties are transcended
To a plane that is frozen in time.
Eyes piercing through each other's souls,
Intakes of breaths become sharper and deeper.
Nervous tingles shocking our bodies.
Memories that never were,
But soon will be,
Wash over us.
Memories that are turned into aspirations:
Aspirations that, as we glance toward each other,
Become fantasies.
Fantasies that we both know,
Will soon become reality.
Pearly whites showing our steadfast hope
Through confident smiles,
Just as our eyes show our burning desire for each other.
Words are stuck in our throats,
As we want that first kiss.
We both see it happening in our minds eye.
The fierce passion,
The wanton desire,
And the all consuming lust,
That we feel for each other is maddening.
All our wants and desires
Are being said without uttering a word.
We have both shared the same vision,
And we know the want we have for each other is real.
We push aside our fear,
Which is replaced by the mutual longing
And need we have for each other.
We are safe within our special moment that will last a lifetime.

I Am...

...a movie critic,
And I hope to be very critical about the movies I love.
And more so about those I despise.
Everyone is a critic.
Unfortunately,
Like the majority of critics,
I don't get paid for my opinion either.
I refuse to suck up for money.
If a movie sucks (any Star Wars movie),
I will tell you,
No holds barred.
I believe
There is a responsibility one has
When sharing your opinion with the world.
And that is to tell the truth.
I have no axe to grind,
Or wheel that needs to be greased.
I won't like a movie,
Just because it's supposed to be great.
All movies have to prove their worth to me.
This will be just one man's opinion,
As honest as he can be.
If anyone has a movie they want me to critique,
Just drop me a line and I'll get to it ASAP.

Here are a few movies and how I would rank them. Do you agree with me? Disagree with me? E-mail me and tell me how you think it should be. It's America. You have the right to be wrong! I've sort of suspended my list as of late. That's why there are really no new movies on the list. I know I've been lax. I might come up with a book of just my movie reviews. Here's my list.

1. Citizen Kane
2. Gone with the Wind
3. Meet Joe Black
4. Zorro, the Gay Blade
5. The King and I
6. Armageddon
7. The Wizard of Oz
8. African Queen
9. Matrix: Reloaded
10. A Time to Kill
11. Titanic
12. Independence Day
13. Leap of Faith
14. The Last Seduction
15. The Rock
16. Die Hard-3
17. Joe's Apartment
18. Mary Poppins
19. Tombstone
20. G.I.Jane
21. Lady and the Tramp
22. 12 Angry Men
23. Rocky - 3
24. The Sum of all Fears
25. Remember the Titans
26. My Fellow Americans
27. Fahrenheit 9/11
28. The Little Mermaid-
29. Finding Nemo
30. The Mask
31. Toy Story-2
32. Hercules
33. Die Hard - 4
34. Aladdin-Disney
35. Toy Story
36. Rocky
37. Ace Ventura
38. How the Grinch stole Christmas-cartoon
39. The Nightmare Before Christmas
40. Little Shop of Horrors-2nd
41. Speed
42. Basic Instinct
43. Happy Gilmore
44. Beverly Hills Cop
45. Monsters Inc.
46. The Rocketeer
47. Arachnophobia
48. Broken Arrow
49. Bull Durham
50. Batman
51. Green Mile
52. The Many Adventures of Winnie The Pooh
53. Jungle Book
54. It's a Mad, Mad, Mad, Mad World
55. Lilo & Stitch
56. True Lies
57. The Last Temptation of Christ
58. Spider-Man-2
59. 101 Dalmatians
60. Catch Me if you Can
61. Bedazzled
62. X-Men-2

63. Big Kahuna
64. X-men Origins - Wolverine
65. Sleeping Beauty
66. Kelly's Heroes
67. How to lose a guy in 10 days
68. Ransom
69. Spider-man
70. Star Trek
71. Mystery Men
72. Frankie and Johnny
73. The Watchmen
74. Billy Elliott
75. Iron Man
76. Die Hard
77. The Naked Gun
78. Bad Boys
79. A Fish Called Wanda
80. The Untouchables
81. The Return of Jafar
82. X-men
83. How the Grinch Stole Christmas-movie
84. The Santa Clause
85. The Aristocats
86. Die Hard-2
87. Mission Impossible
88. Bad Boys-2
89. 21
90. Death to Smoochy
91. The Dark Knight
92. Buzz Lightyear of Star Command
93. Bringing Down the House
94. Bruce Almighty
95. Mulan
96. Willy Wonka
97. Incredible Hulk
98. Chitty Chitty Bang Bang
99. A Bugs Life
100. Beautician and the Beast
101. Alice in Wonderland
102. Paint Your Wagon
103. Rio Lobo
104. Old Yeller
105. Peter Pan
106. Ferngully
107. Fantasia
108. Daredevil
109. Vampires
110. Major League-2
111. The Hangover
112. Scooby-Doo-2
113. Gladiator
114. Superman
115. Duets
116. Fun and Fancy Free-
117. Snow White-goodtimes
118. Bugsy
119. Blown Away
120. 28 Days
121. Mambo Kings
122. Eight-Men-Out
123. Ferngully 2
124. 12 Monkeys
125. Scooby-Doo
126. Pocahontas
127. Little Mermaid-2

128. 10 Items or Less
129. The Adventures of Ichabod and Mr. Toad
130. Speed-2
131. James Bond: Die Another Day
132. Laura Croft: Tomb Raider
133. The Mummy
134. The Recruit
135. Raging Bull
136. 2000 Year Old Man
137. 13th Warrior
138. 3000 Miles to Graceland
139. Flaming Star
140. To Die For
141. Matrix
142. Big Trouble in Little China
143. Bean
144. Billy Madison
145. A Simple Plan
146. The Cable Guy
147. The Waterboy
148. Star Wars-A New Hope
149. Star Wars-The Empire Strikes Back
150. Star Wars-Return of the Jedi
151. Star Wars-The Phantom Menace
152. Star Wars-Attack of the Clones
153. Stars Wars – Revenge of the Sith

I Am...

...a mustard seed
Of faith.
And through me,
All things are possible.
I might be small in stature,
But that is where it stops.
With me,
Size is nothing.
The improbable,
Impossible,
And the extremely unlikely,
Are commonplace to me.
Because if they weren't,
Then I would not be needed.
Ever been scared?
I mean really, really scared?
So scared, you know unless you get a miracle,
You will be dead.
I'm that miracle.
Ever been afraid of a storm?
What about all the things that come with a storm?
Thunder is
Only a loud noise,
But a lightning strike could kill you.
And then there are tornadoes.
We all need help
When those are spinning around us.
Do you think you could ever rebuke a storm?
Not a problem,
If you have me.
You should try it sometime.
It's the easiest way to prove the concept of me.
The next time there is a storm on the horizon,
Just ask God that there would be no damage done
To the surrounding areas,
Be it property or human life.
Ask this in the name of Jesus Christ,
And it will be granted unto you.
No questions asked.
Just a mere mustard seed of faith.
Have you ever brought somebody back from the dead?
Sounds impossible, doesn't it?

It is,
If you don't have me in your life.
How does one acquire me?
All you have to do is ask.
"Ask and thou shalt receive."
Seems easy enough, yes?
You would think more people
Would have me in their lives?
I mean how much simpler does it need to be?
Just ask to have me in your life.
Now asking and receiving does not apply to everything else.
If you ask for a billion dollars,
Which has nothing to do with faith,
Odds are,
You won't be receiving it anytime soon.
God is not a genie,
Nor is he Santa Claus.
God does want to give you everything possible,
To build you up,
But not to tear you down.
The reason you are not a billionaire
Is because God knows you couldn't handle it.
True,
You might be able to handle having the money,
But not the responsibility that comes with it.
Do you see how easy it is with me in your life?
There is another name I go by,
One you might know
But never thought it was me.
I am also the Holy Spirit.
And what better way
Could I be called the Comforter,
Than bringing the comfort of
A mustard seed of faith to you?

I Am...

...a ninja,
and I no longer exist.
But there were the days, my friend
When I struck fear at the mere mention of me.
But today,
I only exist in comic books and movies,
And even then I'm portrayed as a turtle.
There was never a great number of us,
Which is probably how we faded into legend so quickly.
Becoming a legend is easier than one might think.
Just never agree or disagree,
About yourself to anyone.
Just let the rabble assume.
I have a question for you dear reader.
Why are there people trying to teach what I used to do?
You can't teach what I can do.
That is another reason we faded into legend.
These so-called self proclaimed "masters" of the art
Claim to teach ninjitsu.
But why does
It look like something you can learn
In any of those fast food martial arts schools?
How can you teach a person
To sneak up on someone
While being stared at?
Or how do you teach them,
To dodge raindrops?
You can't.
These charlatans will teach you how to use ninja weapons.
This is impossible,
Because we didn't just use a weapon.
Any weapon we incorporated became a part of us.
The sword, bo, sai, or garrote
Took on a life unto its own.
So don't be fooled by these con men that wear a gi.
There is a reason I'm a legend,
And the charlatans are not.

I Am...

...a number.
Which number I am is unimportant,
Because being a number is no different than being anything else.
All numbers have their hopes and dreams.
Let me introduce you to some of my numerical friends.
A side note please;
Zero is not a number.
In reality Zero was something that was invented
In Mesopotamia.
This makes Zero a concept.
The first number to be up is the Number One.
The song says that One is the loneliest number,
But if that's true,
Why does everyone strive to be Number One?
If it's so horrible,
Why does everyone take such pride in shouting,
"We're Number One?"
Isn't that a paradox?
How can "We" be a singular One?
And if it's a plural One,
Is that not the Number Two or more?
My next friend is the Number Two.
The songs says that the Number Two
Is the loneliest number since the number one.
This might be true,
Because just like it is in life,
The only thing worse than being alone,
Is being with someone you can't stand.
But if both entities get along,
You then become a couple.
A couple of what will be determined at a later date.
Next up is three, which is sort of a bitter number
Because it feels like an odd "man" out.
The number Four is very suave.
It likes hearing its name.
Go ahead say its name, F-O-R-E ,
It will slide right off your tongue.
It is the best sounding number there is.
If you notice people ducking around you,
You must have said it a little too loud.
Five is the title number.
There's Five card draw,

30

Or Five work days,
Or FIVE GOLDEN RINGS.
Six is the most sexual number,
Only because it is one vowel away from being Sex.
Some say that Seven is the perfect number,
But every bowler will tell you that Three Hundred is perfect.
Others say that Seven comes Eleven,
Whatever that means.
Eight is the most endless number,
Even though most will agree that Eight is enough.
I say endless because when Eight lays down on its side,
It becomes the symbol of infinity.
The number nine has a very bad inferiority complex.
Who wants to be a Nine when you can be a Ten?
Number nine is the most forgotten number.
It is always standing in the shadow of Ten.
Number nine is the most calculating number,
And the most patient number as well.
It waits for Ten to mess up so it can take Ten's place.
Which leads me to introduce the Number Ten.
This is sometimes a perfect number.
At least Bo Derek thinks it is.
Ten is a very encompassing number.
There is strength in the Number Ten
That you won't find with any other number.
It is the most complete number,
Because it is at the top of everyone's list.
I have never heard of a top nine list.
It's all about being Ten.
I hope this has shown you a new insight
Into the world of numbers.
This now brings me to my number.
Which number am I?
It doesn't really matter,
Because my number is up.

I Am...

...a packet of grape jelly.
I'm a very important part of a nutritious breakfast,
It even says so on my packet.
Especially when you get me on the run.
You pull into your favorite breakfast place,
Ask for a biscuit and jelly,
And a cup of coffee,
And off you go!
You are without a doubt one talented driver.
Not only can you listen to your favorite book on CD,
Talk on your cell phone,
Weave in and out of traffic,
Be able to stop on a dime
Without dropping scalding coffee on yourself,
Foregoing a multi-million dollar lawsuit for yourself;
But you can also open those little packets of me.
And you know how hard it is to open me,
To spread me on your biscuit,
Without missing a beat.
I hate it when you go over a speed bump,
And instead of landing on your biscuit,
I land on the side of the console,
Between the seats.
Oh gravity is such a harsh mistress,
As she drags me down,
At the speed of anxiety,
Only to land on part of,
Last week's dinner of chicken nuggets.
You can't feel the least bit satisfied,
Sitting on a piece of half-chewed chicken nugget
That is turning green with mold.
I pray to the gods of grape above,
And curse the demons of strawberry below
That you'll just stop.
Just stop for 5 minutes and eat your breakfast
So we can both enjoy it.
Is that too much to ask?

I Am...

...a plumber,
And believe me when I say,
There is no difference between shit and poop.
No matter what you call it,
It's still shit.
How can one word be socially acceptable,
But the other word is considered "dirty",
When both words mean the exact same thing?
People are just caught up in the semantics of trivial things.
Being a plumber,
I am your most basic blue-collar worker in the world.
And while I am not a rocket scientist or a slick politician,
I do believe,
My chosen profession is the most valuable around.
I mean, think about it,
Would you like to do what I do each day?
Do you realize how much muck and mire I wade through each day?
Do you know how many times I have to clean my nails each day?
I can't even taste my lunch anymore
When I eat on the job.
I don't travel into the bowels of the earth,
Just the bowels of human kind.
I have to buy new clothes for work every two or three days,
Because of the stench that never can come out.
And yes I do buy the "butt-crack" look for a reason.
It separates me from the world up top.
I used to envy people who work up top, but I don't any longer.
It makes them underestimate me.
They think that they are smarter than me,
Because there is no way they would do what I do.
If they only knew the truth.
If all the plumbers in the world united to form one single union,
We would rule the world
Through the power of the flush.

I Am...

...a poet,
Not a reporter or a journalist.
Some say that seeing is believing,
But in reality,
You have to believe to see.
That is really the truth.
My poems rarely rhyme,
But they reach into the inner sanctum of your soul,
And give you reason to question your life,
And the world around you.
Don't judge my life through the poems you will read.
My poems are just stories
From an idyllic or horrific world
That spans from one end of the cosmos to the other,
Plucking every imaginable emotion and feeling
That is within the perfect realms of my imagination.
I share these things with you
To evoke a response from you.
I attack your thoughts, ideas, beliefs, intelligence, and passions
All at the same time.
You might love what you read,
You might hate that which you have read,
But I can assure you,
You will not be unaffected by these words.
I am a poet,
And that makes me responsible to share all I can
About life as I know it.
I am a poet.
There is no such thing as failure in poetry,
Just a rebirth of ideas that are forged in the fires of imagination.
So in reality we are all poets.
We just express ourselves in different manners.
Some by words,
Either written or typed,
Spoken or in song.
A poet is anybody with an idea,
Who knows how to express that idea.

I Am...

...a police officer.
And my job is not like it's portrayed in the movies,
Or when we were kids,
Playing cops and robbers.
Unfortunately we don't always get the bad guy.
Sometimes we even are the bad guy.
Hard to believe?
Why is it that people always put me on a pedestal?
I am no better than the people I arrest or protect.
As officers we are just a crossbreed of society.
And like any society, 12% of the force is criminal
just like 12% of society is criminal.
Does that make us all bad?
Not at all,
But it does make us all human.
And as a human,
I am subject to the same temptations and faults as everyone else.
As officers be it male of female,
We are tempted in every conceivable way each day,
To look the other way or not to notice a piece of evidence,
Or conveniently lose something important to the case
For a few thousand dollars.
The temptations get more expensive,
As the risks get more dangerous.
For a hundred thousand grand,
We can arrest the wrong person or let the wrong person go free,
On a technicality of course.
For a sexual favor,
The incident in question might never have happened.
I might even be promised everything I ever wanted career wise,
Or family security wise
If I just turn my back on every ethical thing I ever believed in.
These are the temptations police officers are faced with each day.
Who am I tempted by?
What kind of scumbag tempts me most often?
The devil?
If only (s)he really existed for me to blame my weaknesses on.
Money?
Makes the world go around,
And supposedly everybody has their price.
Sex from a beautiful partner?
It is the one subject everybody does lie about.

People in powerful positions?
Who could make your life so much easier if only...
You fill in the blank.
At times all these situations can be very tempting,
But not as tempting as me, myself, and I.
I am my own tempter,
I am the cause of my own downfall,
Just like you are the cause of your own problems.
The human race has been around for thousands of years, right?
It amazes me that we do not live in a perfect, crime free society.
We as adults all know the difference between right and wrong.
So why are there so many people doing wrong out there?
My job should have vanished centuries ago.
But it hasn't, and you have to ask why?
Why am I still needed?
I'm still needed because people
Still choose to make a mistake.
Whether that mistake is taking the law into their own hands,
Carrying out justice due to unwitting passions,
Or just knowingly disregarding the laws.
I bring instant order to a chaotic situation.
I strike fear into the wrongdoers that I apprehend,
And I bring calmness
To those who have been a victim of a senseless act.
I know that I am not above the law nor am I outside of it.
Our motto is "to serve and protect" and I do so proudly.
Being a police officer does not make me your enemy
Any more than it makes me your friend.
Unless you want it to.
You see the choice is yours,
Be my friend and stay within the boundaries of the law,
Or cross those boundaries
And become not just my enemy but public enemy number one.
A word of warning to you,
If you choose the latter,
You are looking at being in a confined space for a very long time.
Either an eight by eight cell shared with some guy named Guido
Who likes the way your butt looks,
Or in a coffin.
The choice is yours.

I Am...

...a politician.
I hope to be a new age politician.
With the dawning of a new millennium
We can do away with old school politics.
No more behind the scenes brokering.
No more scratching someone's back to have your wallet padded.
No more using the blood, sweat and tears of the voters
For the politicians needs instead of the voters needs.
I will be the people's voice
When it comes to health care, civil services, and reducing taxes.
I believe in a socio-democratic society
Where the rich will still be rich,
But there won't be any more poor people.
There will be no homeless or hungry people as well.
Everyone will have the basic necessities,
Including shelter to live in, food to eat, and clothes to wear.
Jobs will be plentiful and the pay will be fair and above scale.
As our children go to better schools that push our young to succeed,
Everyone shall prosper and flourish.
And in doing so, crime will come to a virtual standstill.
Being a new age politician means that the truth will prevail.
I will not debase myself by making empty promises.
And talking of a sacrifice that is never made,
Unless it is made by the under-privileged, will stop immediately.
If sacrifices are needed to be made, then they should start with me.
Isn't the American public tired of seeing politicians grow and prosper
While their cities fall into financial ruin?
What kind of sacrifices will I make to see the dream come true?
I can start by cutting my pay to minimum wage.
I will only get a raise if the economics of the community improves.
I will be punching a time clock
Because you should know when I am really at work.
I might be the public official, but I work for you.
Remember, I want to be a servant of the people, for the people.
That's why it is called public service.
I do this to make my life and my children's lives a better place to be.
I want to bring nobility back to politics.

I Am...

...a polygamist,
And most everyone I know is a polygamist.
I used to be a practicing polygamist,
But the honeybee of love is drawn
To just one flower now.
Are you a polygamist?
If you have had more than one lover or sex partner, you are.
You see,
The Mormons of the Nineteenth Century were just ahead of their time.
And we put their leader,
Joseph Smith, Jr.
To death for his beliefs.
Look at society today.
It's amazing that this country, which was founded on the beliefs
Of religious tolerance, was so intolerant of the Mormons.
We wouldn't let Utah become a state until they changed their religion.
We owe the Mormons an apology - true, it's a bit late,
But better late than never I say.
It is against the law to have more than one wife or husband,
But you can have as many lovers as you can handle.
But doesn't the role of a lover
Take on the role of wife or husband?
True it is the most intimate role,
But it is also the most important role.
Are we not giving of ourselves
When we take our lovers into our midst?
Does this person not become our spouse?
Is there not a responsibility in having a lover?
And if this person is our lover, spouse, mate,
Partner, or even a sperm donor,
Or
A casual hook up sex encounter,
Is he or she not our wife or husband then?
At least to some degree for that some small amount of time,
The two are together?

I Am...

...a procrastinator,

I Am...

...a prostitute,
But then, isn't everybody?
I may sell myself, but
Doesn't everybody who has something to sell do this?
What makes me any different from them?
What makes me any different from you?
Not much I'd wager if the truth is to be told.
Think of all the things people do to get ahead in this world?
I do the same things,
Prostitutes are just a little more carnal and primal that most.
Sometimes it is a little more fun,
A little thrilling, a lot more scary, and usually a lot more disappointing
Than what you had hoped it would be.
The build up is always more fun than the actuality of the situation.
Is what I do wrong, if so, wrong in what regard, I have to ask?
Wrong as in sinful?
I'm as sinful as the next capitalist is.
I run a supply and demand business.
My customers demand a service from me and I supply it.
How is that a sin?
It's an honest days pay for an honest 15 minutes work.
Isn't that what everybody strives for in the work force today?
Aren't I being exploited?
If it pays my bills and buys me the things I want,
Then I guess I am.
But who isn't when they are working for somebody else?
Why is society so much against me?
Why is what I do against the law?
Society comes calling to me, I don't go find them.
All I have to do is smile at a would-be customer,
And he takes it from there. Is that against the law?
The only bad things that are against me:
I get no group health, dental, no 401k, and no early retirement.
All I have going for me is that
Politicians, ugly buildings, and whores all get respect

If they last long enough.
Lucky me.

I Am...

...a shark,
And I have been dubbed
The perfect killing machine.
What a bum rap.
I assure you
That I am perfect in many ways,
But I am not a killing machine.
Oh,
I do kill and quite often.
But only to survive.
Never for sport
Or just because there is nothing else to do.
I do not go kill my father, mother, brother, or sister.
I do not commit genocide against other fish that are weaker than me
Or different from me,
Or don't share the same views of oceanic life as I do.
In reality,
That doesn't sound like a shark at all.
What has been described
Sounds like man.
And we all know
It's man
Who is the perfect killing machine.

I Am...

...a sliding glass door.
I'm always on the outside looking in,
But at the same time
I'm on the inside looking out.
Looking out,
I have a great view of the city I call home.
I'm on top of the bluff so I see most of the action.
I see couples holding hands on the cobblestones below,
As well as children playing with their pets in the park.
On clear days I see all types of boats
Traveling up and down Old Man River,
From tankers to tugboats.
Looking in,
I see a warm, quaint, little world.
She doesn't bother anyone
As she keeps to herself.
I feel we have a lot in common, my mistress and me.
She is always on the inside looking out.
She is a lot like me,
Varying degrees of temperature on the outside,
Ranging from frigidly cold to steamy hot.
While always being nuzzley warm or calmly cool on the inside.
I wonder if she wishes to join the worlds that she spies on?
I don't know what she likes to drink,
But I know that she likes it hot.
I feel the heat of it as she walks by.
I see her sit on the couch
In the unlit efficiency apartment,
She has turned into a home.
As she listens to the wind howl,
Or the rain beat against me.
I see her stare at the ships that are escaping
The ugly realities of the city
For however long they are away from port.
Does she want to escape with them?
She opens me completely
As the wind blows her blonde hair back,
And the mists from the rain lands upon her
As she goes to the railing.
She seems to breathe in the elements about her
As she absorbs all of her surroundings.
The lightning makes funny shadows of her on the far wall,

As the storm picks up its intensity.
Her emotions are all bottled up inside her.
She laughs,
She cries,
She is right on the edge,
Ready to throw herself into the abyss.
She is ready to explode
While the thunder is echoing all around us.
As the storm fades,
She goes back inside soaking wet.
She is as much spent as is the storm.
She curls up on the couch with her hot mug
And just stares out at the openness of the sky.
She is ever the unsatisfied voyeur,
Always on the inside looking out,
Almost afraid of ...
Just like I am.
We are more alike than anyone would guess,
My mistress and her sliding glass door.

I Am...

...a sociopath.
Not a criminal sociopath mind you.
There is a difference.
I've always considered myself a good guy sociopath.
It's kind of funny,
People hear that word and bam,
It has something to do with being bad.
No it doesn't.
It has something to do with being believed.
My fiancé calls me a con man,
But that's not true.
She calls me a gigolo as well.
I deny that with a Cheshire Grin.
I have to deny these things because I want to keep her in my life
For a very long time.
It doesn't matter if I deny them or not,
She has already made up her mind
To the truth she can accept.
Her finding out differently will be a matter of time,
Because time does heal all wounds.
What does being a sociopath mean?
It means I usually get my way.
Not through physical force or mental manipulations.
I do it differently,
I do it by making you the hero.
Everyone wants to be the hero.
Does it not feel good to be the hero,
To make someone's day or life very special?
That is what charm is all about.
I raise you up to be the hero,
I get what I want,
No one gets hurt.
Everything goes my way and I take all the credit
And none of the blame.
What a wonderful plan.
You should try it sometime.

I Am...

...a teacher,
Just like you are.
I have always been a teacher,
Just like you have been.
I was even a teacher when I was a student.
I was teaching my teacher on being a better teacher.
We teach through our words
And through our actions.
You don't have to be a high priced sports figure to be a role model.
Who do we teach most in our lives?
Our unruly children?
Nope.
Our co-workers?
Nope.
Our significant other?
Nope.
The person we teach most in life is us,
And we usually don't listen to ourselves.
We give excellent advice to others
But refuse to listen to it ourselves.
I wonder why?
Are we afraid to succeed?
Are we comfortable with the level we have attained
And are afraid to move forward?
Isn't this like the battered wife syndrome?
I teach because,
If I know something, I want to share it.
Knowledge is power,
And I am power hungry.
We all should be fat with knowledge,
Not by the junk food we cram into our mouths.
We should never become dehydrated of knowledge,
Because we should always be thirsty to learn something new.
And learning something new will change your life
And the lives of those around you.
You'll never say I regret learning that.

I Am...

...a topless dancer,
But that does not mean that I am a whore or prostitute.
I'm dancing my way to a better life.
I can buy nice clothes, a nice car, a nicer place to live.
I make bunches and bunches of money
By showing bare expanses of my skin to men.
Is what I do dirty or sinful?
As much as any other job in America.
I provide a service, not a service of sex,
But a service of giving my patrons a new fantasy.
Is there a dirty side of my job?
Of course there is, but name a job that does not have one?
What service is provided when
A priest molests little boys in the confessional,
Or politicians and judges use their position of power
To seduce would be lovers,
Or teachers who have a straight A, blonde bimbo in their class.
Are these the frequent happenings?
You'd be surprised how frequently these things happen.
Most of the men who come to see me are married.
Does that make me an adulteress or a home-wrecker?
Not at all, remember they came to me, not me to them.
Besides I just give these dirty old men
Something they can't or won't get at home anymore, if ever.
Most of these men offer me the moon.
Have I been tempted to take their offers?
At first maybe, but all I had to do was to look around
At the girls who had taken their offers.
All they gained was losing their self-esteem.
So I dance my patrons into a frenzy,
As my body glides up and down and from side to side.
I laugh and smile at my patrons,
As I hypnotize them into doling out the dollars.
I know this won't last forever.
My beauty will fade and sag.
But while the getting is good,
I'll be getting!

I Am...

...a tornado,
An uncontrollable force of nature, that is me.
Cower before me,
Quake in the path of destruction
That I leave in my wake!
How can you hope to stop me?
Who would dare stand in my way?
You pitiful humans,
Scatter to your storm shelters
And oh so secret hiding spots.
I laugh at your feeble attempts to track
My swath of destruction.
Do you realize how many billions of dollars
You spend on me each year?
And you have no clue about me, do you?
It shouldn't take a rocket scientist to figure it out,
Should it?
I ask you,
When was the last time Wall Street was torn up
By one of my brothers or sisters?
How about one of those giant
Football or baseball coliseums?
Have you ever seen any of those big skyscrapers in Miami
Become damaged by me?
How about one of those casinos in North Mississippi?
That was one of my favorite cutting loose spots,
But no more.
What is so hard to figure out about me?
I can't touch those buildings.
Why you wonder?
Because I run out of gas before I can get there.
How you ask?
Here is the rocket scientist part,
Which we all know Kelly Klemetsrud is not one.
I run on the electromagnetic highway of life.
I can't run over deep foundations
Because they interrupt my highway.
Do you understand?
Trailer parks do not have the same foundation that a skyscraper does.
Now my secret is out,
But there is also another way to stop me.
Just rebuke me.

Sounds simple enough, doesn't it?
God gave you dominion over the Earth.
Do you know what that means?
That means you can assume control of me.
Hard to believe I know,
But it's true.
Why not try it?
Get in the path of me
Or one of my associates and see if you can rebuke me.
What do you have to fear?
God gave you dominion over me,
Right?
God doesn't lie,
Right?
The worst thing that could happen is
You see the Father of us all
Sooner than you planned.
Is that really a bad thing?
So come,
My little fragile friend.
Test your faith against my raw power
And see who'll win.

I Am...

...a tree,
And I have accomplished
What no human has done
In many a millennium.
I am one with the universe,
And I accomplish this through music.
No, not that stuff you humans call music.
The music of we trees is called nature,
And believe me when I say every tree sings in unison
As long as the sun is shining.
I speak for every tree on earth because we share a collective soul.
It might be my words you read, but they are the words of every tree.
You humans used to be able to hear our song,
And sometimes you'd even joined in to sing with us.
That was then, but this is now and you no longer hear us sing,
Both loud and proud.
But every other creature on earth can hear us,
And that's why we are home for so many.
We call these creatures to come home to us with our song.
Today,
Humans and trees have only one thing in common.
Trees and some humans believe in the same creator.
We do have a different name for Him than you do.
But no matter what you call the creator,
A rose by any other name is still a rose,
And the same goes for our creator.
Look how many names your different religions have for him!
It makes no sense to us trees,
Because our one name for the creator
Is accepted by all the trees as truth.
It was a very different world when humans and trees sang in unison.
Can you imagine hearing the deep bass of the mighty oak,
Or the mild falsetto of the weeping willow?
That's when trees were the dominant life force on this planet.
We were ordered to go forth, be fruitful, and multiply first.
That was when the creator made you humans our caretaker.
That was before you fell from grace.
You see humans are the only creatures to fall from grace,
And you guys did it twice.
But to we trees, our world is still perfect.
Until you humans intrude upon us.
Just like in the human world,

Humans are our Satan as well as yours.
Almost over night, you went from being our caretakers to our Satan.
We thank the Creator that some of you humans still cherish us.
But most of you are just plain evil.
You see us standing in your way of progress.
Talk about progress without progression.
Back in the day
Before humans fell from grace the first time,
It was unthinkable to kill a tree.
We were so important to each other's every day life.
Trees helped feed you, clothe you, and provide a shelter for you.
We didn't have to protect you from the elements,
Because there were no dangers to protect you from.
Before you fell the second time,
It never rained.
We lived in a beautiful cloud covered world that was refreshed daily
By a mist rising up from below.
Every creature lived in perfect harmony,
And we all fit together like a perfect puzzle.
Then man fell from grace a second time,
And the Creator in teaching you a lesson, nearly destroyed us all.
It was after the great flood
That our relationship soured and truly ended.
We trees became mere tools for your every whim.
We went from being the dominant life force on this planet
To being cut down,
Chewed up and spat out,
To end up as dust in the wind.
But no matter the damage you humans might inflict upon us,
We still stand proud and tall
Singing praises to our creator.
Maybe the next time you notice one of us,
Or a group of us,
On a mountain side,
Or in a forest,
You'll notice how proud we stand.
And maybe,
Just maybe,
You'll join us in our song.

I Am...

...a twelve-year-old adult.
I know most twelve year olds are considered to be children,
But I am the exception.
Why do I consider myself an adult?
Well,
Name something an adult does that I don't.
I smoke camels,
Not those sissified ultra cigarettes.
I drink hard liquor like Jack Daniels or Jim Beam.
And of course I already mess around with older guys.
They have to be older, because
Guys my age can't really get it up.
I don't belong to any gang.
The only gang I like,
Has a definite bang in it.
Oh sure,
It was scary when I thought I was pregnant.
But hey,
Being pregnant at any age is scary,
Right?
I don't drive yet, but I do know how.
I get high off the good stuff,
Pure Columbian.
I won't buy that cheap Mexican stuff.
You name a pill and I've probably popped it.
Hell...
I even play with women with the best of them.
So you see,
I am a twelve-year-old adult.
But like the song says,
Mammas don't let your babies grow up to be...

Me.

Don't be afraid of saying NO to your child.
If this sounds like your child, be a parent and not a friend.
Children must have boundaries,
So they know the consequences of crossing said boundaries.

51

I Am...

...a used car salesman.
And is this not a glorious day?
In fact,
Is this not the most perfect day
That you have ever been a part of?
Why is today so perfect, you ask?
Well,
The sun is shining,
Everyone is smiling,
And you have come to me to buy a new, previously owned car.
And not just any previously owned car,
But the perfect previously owned car for you.
Are you looking for something sporty?
I knew it.
I have something very, very special for you.
I have a limited edition,
Supercharged,
Four on the floor,
Neon plaid,
Almost turbo charged,
Made in America,
GMC Pacer.
It's a classic.
This is a once in a lifetime car,
And it car will fit you like a glove.
You will look totally rad in this car.
My job is not just to move cars,
But to make you feel good,
And look even better, because of
Buying a previously owned car from me.
And if you are not happy,
Then I'm not happy.
It's all about trust, right?
Is that not the most important element of any relationship?
I need you to trust me,
And in that trust we will both find happiness.

I Am...

...a virgin,
And I'm proud of it, too.
For an adult,
Virginity is all about attitude,
Not sexual experience.
I've had plenty of sex partners,
But never a lover,
Until now:
Until Sabra.
We are going to be married in February of 2002.
Virginity is an age of innocence
Within all of us.
And with Sabra,
I have reclaimed my innocence
Just like she has with me.
I am experiencing feelings I either thought
Were dead or long dormant within me.
I almost cried when I gave her
The engagement ring.
Why?
Because, it made me happy knowing that it made her happy.
Isn't that what losing your virginity is all about?
Finding a lover that you can give all your love to.
Giving of yourself just to one person.
The right one person?
You are not just giving your body to your lover,
But you giving your soul.
The two becoming one,
To share yours with hers.
And when you give up that soul to share with another,
That is when you lose your virginity to that person
Who is now your lover.
Sex is just a physical exercise,
While making love is exercising of your soul.

I Am...

...a Warrior.
Do you know what that means?
It means I do not stop fighting
Until there is no one left to fight.
Some people get a warrior
Confused with a soldier.
There is a big difference:
A soldier fights out of a sense of duty,
While a warrior fights for what (s)he believes in.
A soldier can be a warrior,
But a warrior can never be a soldier.
I am not a soldier:
Never had the idea of being one.
Being a soldier is an honorable way of life,
But not for a true warrior.
Ever ready to fight the never-ending battle,
Of truth,
Justice,
And my way of thinking.
Why do I fight for my way of thinking?
Because my way of thinking is the right way.
I know that might not be proper English,
But there is a difference between being correct,
And in being right.
And I know that my way of thinking is right.
If you do not believe in yourself,
How do you expect others
To follow your example?
Mistakes are made,
But they are resolved,
Not brushed aside,
Or covered up.
What is the difference between me and a soldier?
A soldier has everything issued to him,
From the clothes (s)he wears,
To the weapon (s)he uses.
A warrior creates their own setting,
And the weapon in question is the warrior him or herself.
I use my wits,
Brains,
And experience
As my weapons of choice.

I have no need of knives or firearms.
A soldier always has to answer to somebody;
A warrior answers to nobody but to himself and his God.
I don't waste my time
Trying to diplomatically find a solution.
When the call of battle is sounded,
It can only mean one thing.
Someone is going to be hurting,
And I also know that someone won't be me.
When I fight my battles,
I know I will fight until my dying breath.
I don't know how to give up.
I might die,
But I know my sacrifice
Will not be in vain.
Because I know damn well
I won't be dying alone.
But have you seen what happens
To soldiers without a cause to fight for?
They either become politicians,
Or diplomats,
And fight for their own agendas.
And this is almost criminal,
Especially under the disguise of wanting to help others.
Or they may become totally lost.
Can a warrior ever find peace
If (s)he is not dead?
Is there not a serene peace on the battlefield,
No matter how loud and chaotic it might be?
I think of two things
When there is no battle to fight:
I'm in heaven,
And this is paradise all around me.
Or,
The bastards have won,
And I've lost my mind.

But I know in my mind
The bastards will never win.

I Am...

...a window to your soul.
I'm the second most intimate act there is.
With me,
The truth is revealed.
I can tell your passions,
And your falsehoods.
I can tell if you got to,
Have to,
Or if you even wanted to.
Or, if you didn't want to at all.
I can tell how full of promise you will be,
Or how empty that promise is going to be.
I'm always at the beginning,
But never at the end.
You love everything I start,
And hate when there's nothing left of me.
I'm that irresistible impulse,
That you can't break away from.
I'm the most desired addiction there is,
And I'm all legal, too.
I can be the start on the road
To a living hell,
Or to a glorious paradise.
Something this complex
Was never so simple.
So simple...

As a kiss.

I Am...

...a winner.
Which is a lot better than being the alternative.
Let me tell you,
Winning is so easy
It makes me wonder
Why there aren't more of us.
Do you know what is easier than being a winner?
Being a failure,
Giving up,
Or turning your back on your morals and principles.
Those things are even easier than winning.
Winning is like a row of dominos:
Once you set everything up,
It all falls into place.
Easy as pie.
It doesn't take anything special to be a winner,
It really doesn't.
You already have what it takes.
All it takes is sacrifice.
You can do that can't you?
What are you willing to sacrifice to be me?
Understand this please,
The bigger the sacrifice,
The bigger the prize.
At least,
That's what you will tell yourself
To justify your sacrifice.
Let's just hope
That those you've sacrificed
Will be just as understanding.
If you're going to sacrifice
All that you have
To get what you want.
Make sure, the sacrifice
Is not your soul,
That is.

I Am...

...afraid.
I have been for most of my life.
Life has always been so harsh for me,
From being molested as a child
To being raped as a teenager.
On to being physically abused over and over again;
By not just my husband of many years,
But by my children, as well.
I'm afraid,
Because I know I will be punished.
I deserve to be punished.
Nothing seems to go my way.
I know that when people are happy,
They are supposed to have a warm, giddy feeling about them.
I don't ever have that feeling.
Most times, I'm just cold.
Not just bbbrrrr cold, but, shiver-me-timbers type cold.
I also know that if you are cold,
You are probably not very happy.
Most people think Hell is all fire and brimstone.
Not my Hell.
My Hell is all cold.
I also have noticed that the colder I feel,
The less faith I have
In God, myself, my life.
Everything seems so chaotic.
I am truly a Doubting Thomas, and nobody knows it.
I would like to think that I put on a really good show.
And that's exactly what it is, just a really good show
That fools everybody but me. And, I hate myself for it.
I know God will punish me for the deceptions I make,
Even if I am the only one being deceived.
I'm so afraid of God, myself, and my life.
I know God is going to punish me for my past sins:
For all those sins I forgot to ask forgiveness for.
My God is an angry God,
Who demands we obey Him without question.
Will I be turned into a pillar of salt for not obeying Him?
I'm so afraid, I know I have to be punished
And I deserve to be punished.
Why do you think I cut myself?
Maybe God won't punish me so severely

If I go ahead and punish myself.
I like to see the blood pulse from my wounds.
Isn't justice being done with each drop of blood?
Can I find absolution in my blood?
Look at all of the people I have not made happy.
Why shouldn't God punish me?
Everyone else already does.
I'm so afraid to die,
But I'm even more afraid to live life to the fullest.
I'm afraid of what God will do to me if I don't obey Him.
Will He take one or all of my children to be back with Him?
Will He cause my soul-mate to not be in love with me anymore?
Will I lose my job and then my livelihood?
What then becomes of my children?
Will I be seen as an unfit parent and have them taken from me?
Will my children grow up thinking I have abandoned them?
I'm so afraid and so cold. So very, very cold.
What if I cut myself too deep?
What if I end it with just one deep slash?
Then, I guess I'll be eternally punished.
I'm so alone in my fear.
IS THERE ANYONE OUT THERE?
Do you hear my pleas, but won't let me in?
Is there no room for me at the inn?
I know I'm alone, because all I hear about me
Are the echoes of my anguished cries.
Does anyone else have these fears?
Fears
Fears
Fears.
Does anybody else share these fears?
Fears
Fears
Fears.
The echoes never die down.
They are always there just like my fears,
Fears
Fears
Fears.

I Am...

...all about me.
This is how I live my life.
In every day
And in every way.
Boy, doesn't that sound selfish?
I'm sure it does,
If you don't have a life worth living.
I refuse to be just another faceless droid
In a wave of endless beings
Waiting for the right time to come along.
I believe in Carpe Diem -
Seize the day.
Time waits for no man,
And neither does life.
Because it continues
Whether we are a part of it or not.
Life just keeps rolling right along.
Some people refuse to live life to its fullest potential,
Because they want a better life in the next one.
What a crock!
What a sin!
Not to live this life to its fullest potential
In the hope that
Those in question will be rewarded exponentially.
Don't they understand that this is their end reward?
Of all those hundreds of thousands of sperm,
We are the ones that reached the egg first.
We have been rewarded with a life of our very own
To live to it's fullest potential.
And by doing so,
We are giving thanks and praise to our creator all at the same time.
I'm God's favorite child,
Just like you are.
I live every day like I have just won the lottery.
And if I'm lucky enough to have someone new in my life,
Then I can share my world with them.
And by doing so,
Partake in their world, as well.
Pity the person who is no wiser than they were yesterday:
They are definitely poorer for it.
In my world,
It's all about me.

It has to be.
Just like it's all about you, the reader, in your world.
Wait!
Stop the presses!
What about our children?
Mine and yours?
Everybody has a place in everybody's world.
It goes without saying that
Children share a special place in each of our lives.
We gain immortality through our children,
Because as long as they live and their children live,
We are able to live through them.
We all have the usually thankless job of molding our children's lives.
Molding their lives so that they can become self sufficient,
So they can live in a world that is all about them.
But instead of molding their lives,
Give them a good foundation of great memories
To build their life upon.
Another way to put it :
It's all about me in my world,
Just like it is all about you in your world.
Don't waste your time not living life to its fullest.
Because if you aren't doing that,
Then you are truly wasting your life.

I Am...

...alone,
And loneliness is my sworn enemy.
Man, be it male or female,
Is not meant to be alone.
Have you ever been alone?
Most people will say yes.
But when you press the subject,
It becomes quite clear that they haven't.
I have been alone my friend.
I know loneliness all too well.
And she is a very stern mistress.
If loneliness were a woman we would be the most intimate of lovers.
Love and Hate are levels of reality that I could never really grasp.
Because the concept always took something I never had:
A partner.
That's why loneliness is almost an extension of my being.
Do you understand what loneliness is all about?
Have you ever been hungry? Really, really hungry?
You know that gnawing feeling you get,
When the bile is building up in the pit of your stomach?
You'd even trade your birthright to your younger brother
To get your hunger sated.
That is loneliness.
Loneliness is very greedy and is never at peace.
It's selfishness turns your prime and virile self
Into just an apparition of that former self.
You will become desperate, and in your desperation,
Will find out what fear is all about.
You'll sell your soul to not be lonely, and in doing so,
You'll end up twice as lonely.
Loneliness is a predator
That swallows up all hope and brightness within you.
The fear of becoming lonely is very powerful,
Because it drowns out all common sense.
I should know. Because it does this to me.
I try to fight against being lonely and in doing so,
I fight right into its grasp.
The harder I fight it the more elusive my goal becomes,
And the more desperate I get.
Which just makes me that much more lonely.
Loneliness is like an itch that can never be scratched.
I've never seen the movie

Or even understood the title.
But in this instance,
It sort of makes sense:
Loneliness is like a seven-year itch.
I sometimes think
That the reason I'm so lonely,
Is that I'm serving some type of penance
Because I've had no respect
For the women I knew early in my adulthood.
Then it hits me.
Maybe I'm serving my penance,
Because I have no respect for myself?
I can't allow my loneliness
To turn into despair.
Despair happens
When all hope is gone,
And you just give up on yourself
And everything around you.
Never give up.
If you give up,
You die.
Just relax,
Take a few deep breaths,
And enjoy the life you have been granted.
There is a cosmic balance at work:
Everything that has been subtracted from your life
Will eventually be added back.
So,
No matter how bad it gets,
And it might get even worse,
It will get better.
Because, God will not let something
Happen in your life
That you can't handle.

Re-read those last three lines.

I feel better,
Don't you?

I Am...

...alone in a crowd.
Yet,
There is no one around me.
Except for
Everyone I have ever known.
"Leave me alone", I plead to them.
The echoes of my screams
Are deafening to me.
No one listens to me.
I'm being ignored yet again.
I hate being ignored!
Why can't they just ignore me
By leaving me alone?
They are so close to me,
Just pressing into me,
Invading my personal space.
Please,
Leave me alone.
I'm choking on the smell
Of their perfume,
The turkey sandwich they had for lunch,
Their sweat,
Their breath,
Their pheromones.
It's so nauseating,
But I can't throw up.
If I do,
It's just dry heaves.
God!
Get them to leave me alone!
I don't need them.
I don't need anybody.
Because, I have all of you to keep me company,
As long as you just leave me alone.
I'm so scared.
Fear rules my life.
I fear them,
I fear you,
I even fear myself.
The list of fears goes on forever it seems.
I'm afraid to die,
Afraid to live,

Afraid of my past,
Afraid of my future,
As well as my present.
My fears are held together,
Quite nicely I might add,
By the guilt that comes with each fear.
This is compounded by the sadness
That fits over my life,
Like a veil,
Or death shroud, maybe.
To signify an ending?
Or maybe like a marriage veil,
To signify a new beginning.
Whatever it is,
It's smothering me.
Which scares me.
I feel like I'm drowning
In my own despair.
Focus.
Stay calm.
How much further until the surface?
I don't want to die,
But I'm afraid to live.
Why can't the pain
Just ignore me,
Like everyone else does?
I scream,
I cry,
But they can't hear me.
I'm all alone.

I Am...

...an addict.
Is that such a surprise?
Are you not an addict?
Aren't we all addicted to something?
From biting our fingernails,
Picking our noses,
And having that cup of coffee in the mornings,
To that cigarette after a good romp in bed,
Or selling ourselves as a sex object for our next fix.
Addictions come in so many shapes and sizes.
Does it have to be illegal to be addictive?
It can be very legal,
And just as harmful and deadly as something illegal.
Nose spray is very legal,
(My lawyers say I cannot name the brand in question,
So you pick a brand, you probably won't be wrong)
But just as addictive as crack cocaine.
Aren't we all addicted to breathing?
And since nose spray helps clear your nasal passages to breathe,
You get hooked, spending five to seven dollars on a bottle of the stuff.
Then you always need a bottle at home.
By your bed,
In the bathroom,
Near your computer,
Plus one everywhere else.
In your car,
Two at work,
And in your coat pockets.
People get accustomed to seeing you snorting these bottles down.
And the women go crazy, seeing a man
Snorting half a bottle of nose spray up his nose.
But hey,
This is all legal.
What's the down side?
Nose spray destroys your sense of smell.
A small price to pay for breathing though,
Yes?
Addictions are born through timing and repetition.
They don't just happen:
They are created.
Addictions start out innocently enough.
A drink here,

A snort there,
And the realization to ourselves
That we can quit at anytime.
Hey, this is fun!!
We are in control.
I'm in control!
This stuff isn't so bad!
Everything is copacetic.
So, what is everyone so worried about?
An addiction creeps up on us a little bit at a time.
A puff here,
A hit there,
And the belief that we can quit at anytime we want.
Wow! This is easy.
NOOOOOOO problem here.
An addiction is like a snowball, that rolls down a mountain.
It starts small,
But as you let it go unchecked, it will consume you.
For that is the nature of the beast!
It will roll over all of your hopes and dreams.
And probably take with it, the hopes and dreams
Of the ones you love the most.
It always starts out small:
A caress here,
A fantasy fulfilled there.
And the belief within, that we can quit at anytime.
Then Bam!!
Just as fast as I climbed to the top,
Everything starts spinning into a kaleidoscope of fear and horror.
All I want now is to be left alone, without ever being by myself.
Where is all of that attention I craved,
And the glamour that used to be so easy to obtain?
Now, it's a groan here, a sob there, and the realization.
That I could never quit, or assume control,
Of whatever I took for granted,
And treated like a child's toy or game.
Is this how it ends?
Is it?
Only you can decide that!
Only you.

I Am...

...an angel.
And so are you.
We are all angels.
How can this be?
I thought angels were spiritual creatures.
They are servants to God.
But are we not all just a servant of God?
When you are in a bind and are helped out by a complete stranger,
The person that helped you is an angel.
There is an angel inside each of us.
Which is our spiritual side
That many are not even aware exists.
Before the fall of man,
We were all in touch with our spirituality.
We were able to see things and to communicate.
Not just in three dimensions,
But in a fourth and fifth dimension as well.
Our Spirituality is an access to these other dimensions.
When we are in need of help,
Our spiritual form sends out a cry for help,
that is answered by another spiritual being.
Those who ignore or refuse our cries
Are just fallen angels.
So the next time someone helps you out of a jam,
Just realize,
You are in the company of angels.

I Am...

...an athlete.
And a sportsman
In the truest sense of the word.
But,
Agents aren't lining up at my door
To sign me to million dollar contracts.
Nobody wants me to endorse their product.
I can't run a 4.5 forty-yard dash.
I can't slam dunk the final basket or make that crucial three-pointer
With .02 seconds left.
Or, with two on, with two outs in the bottom of the ninth,
I will not be called upon to get the game winning run,
Or to strikeout the opposing batter.
I won't be able to return a kick-off 97 yards for a touchdown.
Even though I might have the physical skills to drive a car,
I do not possess the physical fortitude
To drive a car for hours at a high speed.
The coach on my team will never be ejected for arguing
Over balls and strikes.
And none of my teammates will ever
Put themselves above their team.
The sports that I play in, are team sports.
Even if we compete by ourselves
We are never alone.
I play for the love of the game,
And for the sake of pure enjoyment.
I play to revel in the cheers that cascade
From friends, family, and even opponents.
I am an athlete for The Special Olympics.
Come join me in the celebration of life.
Whether we win or lose,
We all still win.
Because our efforts are pure,
And so is our intent to
Become one with the game.
I am a Special Olympics Athlete,
And no matter the outcome of the contest,
Everyone always wins.

I Am...

...an electrician.
And I empower the world.
Is this not the coolest job in the world, to have?
Not too many people could live their lives
Without me doing my job.
Is my job dangerous?
Very much so, but probably no more than your job,
If you get careless with it.
You realize that more things run on electricity,
Than all the other fuels combined?
That's because all living things run on electricity.
Okay,
Electrical impulses maybe, but still electricity.
Society is always looking for a new fuel source.
But, the best undiscovered fuel source
Has always been right under our noses.
We are that fuel source,
You,
Me,
And everyone else in the world.
Maybe that's how the ancient druids or pharaohs got things done.
They knew how to tap into and store their electrical output.
Today's society,
Which we are all part of,
Has just forgotten how to tap into that potential.
But,I bet it's still there, just waiting for us to use it.
Do you know how many electrical impulses
Your body sends out each day?
At least 43,200,000 per day, I'm sure.
I wonder how much energy one person could generate?
Wouldn't it be neat,
If we could somehow
Stick our finger into a plug,
And heat or cool our house for a day?
Sounds crazy I know,
But today's crazy ideas
Are tomorrow's realities.

I Am...

...an err in judgment.
You know,
One of those instances that can change your life.
Or at least
Haunt you for all of your days.
Picture this:
I'm in my early thirties,
Divorced,
And wanting to give my life a good jumpstart.
I have more money than a politician.
I went to LA to start a new life,
And met an ex-wife of a famous baseball player.
She even threw a party
In my honor!!
We were really clicking, and
I was hobnobbing with the rich and famous
Out on the West Coast.
Of course, this has-been, ex-ball player was there.
I'm sure you've heard of him;
All he talked about was being back in the "day".
This guy would not shut up
About how big, bad, and tough he was
And supposedly is.
He even had a gun and was showing it off
To whoever would watch and listen to him.
Then he starts posing with this gun he has,
Like he's James Bond or something.
He even gave me the gun, to hold for him.
What a bastard!
Like I was some sort of maitre d'.
Then without a moments hesitation,
I pointed his gun at him and squeezed off six shots:
Bam..!!

Bam..!!   Bam..!!
Bam..!!   Bam..!!

Bam..!!
All in a nice tight circle.
That puts an end
To Mr. Life of the Party.
Like the song says:
It's my party
And I'll kill the bastard if I want to.

71

That'll teach him to hand a gun to someone he doesn't know.
You should have seen the look on his face
When I fired that first shot!
Ha!
It was priceless!
Let's see how tough you are now,
You Don Johnson, Miami Vice reject!
I think he peed his pants!
The rest of the guests
Were shocked into silence.
Like this stuff didn't happened everyday in LA?
He shouldn't have given me his gun.
I wanted to start a new life:
And if the gun had been loaded,
I would have.
At the California State Penitentiary,
For Murder
In the first degree.
All for the sake of
An err in judgment.

I Am...

...an Indian.
And you have no idea
What that actually means.
This poem will not deal with all the injustices
We Indians have had to endure
Since the Beginning of time.
No.
This poem is about
What being an Indian means.
It means we were first.
First born.
First here.
First to stand upright on Mother Earth.
First in this nation that you call America.
And first in most countries across this planet.
Does this surprise you?
There was a time on this planet
When there were just four races of men.
Four races,
Not the multitude of races we have today.
There were the Indians.
And we were first in this world.
Then the Black man,
Then the Oriental man,
And last,
The White man cometh.
A lot of races have spawned from these four:
From the White man
Has come only the White man.
I guess enough was enough.
The Oriental man spawned
Chinese,
Japanese,
And all of those far-east races.
The Black man
Was the second race to tread upon our Earth.
He gave birth to scores of races,
Which mostly are now extinct.
Extinct, because the Black man was too trusting.
And too hungry for love.
Love of Knowledge.
And we all know that love is blind.

Blind to other races that eventually slaughtered them.
Out of jealousy or fear.
We Indians have given birth to more races
Than the other three original races combined.
We gave birth to the
Eskimo's,
Spaniards,
Central and South American Indians,
Indians out of India,
As well as
The Middle-east.
These include:
Israelites,
Egyptians,
Iranians,
Iraqis,
Kuwaitis,
Shiites,
And all of the Muslim world.
The Mediterranean area,
Asia,
And Southern Europe,
All originate from Indians.
They are all brothers,
In love and war.
Which they constantly wage against each other.
If the Hebrew Indians in your Bible had traveled and explored,
Noah would have had four sons instead of three.
They did not realize
Oriental people existed in the world.
That's why, in your Bible,
Noah had only three sons instead of four.
So you see,
We are the origin of Mankind,
And your origin comes from us.

I Am...

...anal.
No, I'm not.
But I would really like to be.
When we think of something anal,
I can't imagine that "neat and orderly" springs to mind.
Instead,
Something dark and dank, that smells a whole lot like,
You know,
Something from the anus.
Talk about a bizarre sense of humor.
You want to have fun?
Tell your Mother-in-Law she's very anal
And compliment her on it.
Talk about a left handed compliment.
You compliment her,
You shock her,
You stun the people around her,
Because you said the word anal in front of her.
And she is the butt of your joke,
Which was always meant as a compliment;
In a left handed sort of way.
Talk about a win-win situation.
Oh Happy Day!
Sing it with me!

I Am...

...Busy, busy, busy.
I have a thousand things to do today.
Go to Wally World,
Pay the cable bill,
Go to the gas station,
Stop by the drug store for medicine,
And pick up pizza for dinner.
And I get to go to all these places
With my five & seven year old girls.
Not that I mind, because we have a blast!
Let me tell you,
They can be as opposite as night is to day.
But when they ride in the car with me,
They are like long lost friends
Who have just rediscovered themselves.
We play games:
Such as I Spy,
And tongue-twisters.
And of course we sing songs.
Since I only know three songs,
Those are pretty much the only ones we sing.
But hey,
They are three great songs.
We start off by me singing
I Love you,
Then the girls chime in,
And we love you.
Then we all sing,
So let's wallah-wallah down by the mango tree.
I tell my girls,
"That's the first song you guys ever learned."
Bridgette,
My seven year old says,
"I thought it was Miami Dolphins."
I go no,
That was the second song.
To which we all break into a rousing chorus of,
Miami Dolphins,
Miami Dolphins,
Miami Dolphins number one!
They're on the ground,
Or in the Air,

They're always in Control!
And when you say Miami,
You're talking Superbowl!
I find a parking space,
Just down the street from the Drug store.
I need to race in
And pick up some medicine.
Kelleigh-Jaymes,
My five year old says,
"Let's sing
I've been working on the railroad",
Which causes them to sing as loud
as humanly possible.
I tell them,
"I'll be right back and to stay in the car."
We've done this same thing a hundred different times.
They're good girls,and
They've never disobeyed me.
They are usually too enthralled in playing with each other
To even know I've left the car.
This is a safe neighborhood.
There is hardly any crime of any kind.
I rush into the store, where it takes a bit longer than I thought.
And then I rush out,
Hoping no one has to go to the bathroom too badly.
A crowd has gathered around a car.
There are flashing lights from a police car.
Must have been an accident.
I hope no one is hurt.
I hurry up the sidewalk, and hear
That there is a broken car window.
A police officer is there,
Talking to some of the crowd.
Some People are pointing up the street,
While others are pointing down the street.
Oh My Gosh,
That's my car with the broken passenger side window!
That's my car that people have gathered around!
That's my car.
And, it doesn't have two little girls in the back seat playing!
"Where are my little girls?", I scream!
The police officer asks me if this is my car.
I say yes, But where are my girls?
That's when I get,
All at the same time,

A different version of events
From every person who has gathered around my car.
"Where are my girls?" I scream.
Why didn't anyone stop the guy who did this?
Did anyone get a look at the guy?
How can someone just bash in a car window
On a busy street.
And take two little girls out of the back seat,
Without anyone noticing, I scream!?!
My heart sinks.
I just know that my babies have been taken
By some depraved lunatic.
And the chances are that
I'll never see my little girls again.
"This is just a nightmare"!
I wake up saying,
"This IS just a nightmare"!
Thank you God!
Even though I live in a relatively crime free area,
I never believed crimes of this nature could take place.
I'm sure they do.
But not in rural,
Small town America.
This happens to people who don't care about their kids.
Not to people who love & adore their children.
This happens to other people,
But, not to me!
Or so I thought.
I'm glad I woke up,
And this dream did not become a reality.
I'm glad that God taught me this lesson
In my sleep instead of being awake!
No matter where I go now,
My babies come inside with me every time.
No exceptions!
Make sure
Your babies do too!

I Am...

...can you guess?
Maybe I'm the storm on the horizon,
A plethora of things yet to unfold.
Moving at the speed of anxiety,
I encompass the entire spectrum of life.
From the filthy rich,
To the starving and wretched poor.
I am evil,
Pure evil.
Simple
And unadulterated.
I am also
Unforgiving,
Ruthless,
Indifferent,
Uncaring,
And my rage knows no boundaries.
I reek of sloth and greed,
As I dance on the blood of innocence.
Do I sound familiar?
Who am I?
You know me.
Like the song says,
Say my name!
Say my name!
Do you need another hint?
I cry no tears for the dead.
I neither give comfort to the downtrodden,
Nor do I give freely of myself,
Except, when I can profit from it.
I try to have my cake and eat it too.
I always put myself first.
Who am I?
You know it,
Say my name!
I get away with things
That you can only dream of getting away with.
I maim, murder, and rape the unsuspecting,
All with the greatest of ease.
I am the bane of humankind.
Surely by now you know who I am?
My name must be on the tip of your tongue.

The suspense must be killing you.
I know that you know me.
Say my name!
I am...
Drum roll please,
Ta-Da!!
I am
SATAN...
Ruler of the fiery pits of Hell,
The Crown Prince of Darkness,
As well as
The Prince of Lies.
Does that satisfy your smug sense of self-righteousness?
Nothing can get by you,
Oh aged, wise one.
Do you have any sympathy for me?
I have some for you.
You silly person.
Silly, Silly Person,
I am not Satan,
I am you.
And you are all that I have described.
I am everyone who has ever existed,
Or ever will be born.
Why pin your fallibilities on a myth?
Every evil act in the world
Is committed by man.
Be it male or female:
It is still man who does everything evil.
Tell me, or better yet, show me one act,
Be it good, bad,
Or indifferent
That Satan has supposedly committed.
You can't do it.
The only thing satanic in this world is us.
We are Satan.
Now that you know yourself,
What will you do?
Ignorance once dispelled,
Cannot be reclaimed.

I Am...

...death,
And guess what?
HAHAHAHAHAHAHAHAHAHAHAHAHAHAHAHAHAHAHAHAHAHAHAHAHAHA,
(In the most maniacal laugh possible)
I'm coming to get you,
And him,
And her,
And everybody you know,
Care for,
Or have
Ever loved,
Ignored,
Or even hated.
I am the final chapter in your book of life.
And believe me when I say this.
There is no sequel planned.
That is the reason you fear me.
Plain and simple.
Because, one day
You are here on this earthly plane
Complaining about your ungrateful children,
A dead-end job,
Your significant other, or
Not being significant enough.
And then
The next day,
You aren't.
I guess that does sound pretty scary.
Boo!
HAHAHAHA!!!
Why do I laugh at you,
You may ask?
Because I'm not the one you should be afraid of.
Did you know that there are actually people
Out there in the real world
Who aren't really afraid of me?
Do you know what the difference is
Between those people and you?

And religion has nothing to do with me.
If you are a born again Christian,
Great!

If you aren't,
Hey,
No problem.
I'm still coming for you.
HAHAHAHAHA!!
Some people think they might wake up in a better place after they die,
Some a worse.
But Heaven or Hell has nothing to do with me.
My job is to make sure that
You don't wake up here,
On this earthly plane.
Wow!
I'm scaring myself, here.
What if I die?
Can death die?
But, back to those people
Who have no fear of me.
You could be one of those people.
Want to know how?
The people most afraid of me
Are those people
Who are most afraid to live.
I am just an easy cop-out fear for them.
It sounds pretty stupid to say that you are afraid of life and living.
But it's perfectly normal to say you are
Scared of death and dying.
Right?
Only to those who share your fear.
Let me tell you a secret.
Bring me closer to you,
Read these next words carefully and slowly.
Once you conquer your fear of
Life and living,
You won't have a fear of
Death and dying.
It's as simple as that.
Live your life without any regrets,
Living to the fullest extent possible.
And when I come for you,
You will welcome me
Instead of fear me.

I Am...

...escaping.
My face is flushed, red.
My breath is haggard.
I am running and racing for my life.
Where am I?
I have no idea.
Some sort of castle or mansion, I assume.
Lord, this place is huge.
To top it off, my tormentor is a clown.
Not Bozo or Ronald mind you;
But a clown who has escaped from the psycho circus.
I run up very steep and narrow stairs.
One dark spiral staircase after another, until I finally reach the top.
My heart is about to burst through my chest.
Why am I running up these stairs, in stark terror?
Up, up, up I go. Instead of out, out, out,
Where freedom screams for me.
I'm on the roof, on a patio of sorts:
I see the circus,
Where my last memory remains, about 5 miles away.
My heart is beating,
Almost as loud as that damn clown is laughing.
That hysterical clown.
He shuffles forward with heavy steps
As I feel my hot, sticky, sweat sliding down my back.
The demonic clown continues to laugh:
As I scream
Praying that someone will hear and rescue me.
I look for an escape.
I'm trapped.
I'm screaming like a banshee. But to no avail.
No one can hear me.
My throat is raw from screaming.
I not only see the distorted clown,
But the shroud of death that hangs over him.
There is no place else to run.
And, I'm too weak to fight.
Oh God, I don't want to die.
I want to pass out, but I must continue on.
Go, go, go...
Oh Damn.
I'm backed up to the edge of the roof as close as I can be.

I will not fall. I will not fall.
Steady, just don't look down.
The leering clown is so close to me
That I can smell his greasy face paint.
The frenzied clown makes his move, and I move like lightning.
Some would call it courageous.
But I know that its really desperation.
I jump from the roof,
Grab the banner and slam myself into the wall that is
Three stories below, where I fall the rest of the way down.
I pick up my very bruised body, and become the marathon man I am.
I do the 5 miles in just one stride.
Go, Speed Racer, go.
I cannot stop, and I will not rest.
I'm almost there, I'm almost safe.
The only thing keeping pace with me is that insane clown.
I'm here, but I'm not safe.
I'm in my car.
About damn time!
Miraculously I find my keys,
But of course the car won't start.
It will not start.
It will not start.
It will not start.
I pray to the Gods above
And curse the Devil below.
I see that hideous clown in my rear-view mirror getting closer.
I keep the gears grinding,
As I start to cry a slow, sorrowful, sob.
The car finally starts and the tires screech,
As I race away from that grisly clown.
He gives a loud pot-bellied laugh:
A laugh that echoes
Throughout time and space.
It reminds me that we must meet again.
I know we are fated to meet again.
Over and Over again,
Till death do us part.

I Am...

...fat,
But, does that make me
Any less human than you?
Fat by definition,
Is twenty pounds over your ideal body weight.
But if you look around you,
Almost everyone is fat.
And if you are thirty plus pounds,
You are also obese.
I bet, even you could afford to lose a few pounds.
Let's face it: It's the nature of the beast.
Remember a few centuries ago
When being portly was in vogue.
If you don't believe me,
Go to any museum.
You'll see that most paintings from that era
Have large women in them.
If not large,
Then at least fleshy.
These women were not considered fat.
But, men that same size were.
(Big sigh)
Some men like a pregnant-looking woman.
But no woman
Likes a pregnant-looking man.
In today's world,
Fat is a sin.
A minor sin,
But still a sin,
While being obese is just plain hideous.
And if you pick up any magazine,
You might see a pudgy woman
Selling X-large clothes,
But you will rarely see an actual fat lady
Selling clothes that she could or would wear.
And you never see an obese lady or man selling anything.
Most models are skinny-minnies. And our society drinks it up.
Do you realize that our nation as a whole,
Spend so much money on diet products in a year,
That we could probably find a cure for cancer,
Or for Hiv/Aids.
And this is the most ironic of all,

We could even end hunger in most third world nations?!
I'm serious.
The diet industry is a multi-billion,
Maybe even, a multi-trillion dollar business.
Why?
Why are we so intent on capturing
A part of our youth
That we can never get back,
Even if we do lose the desired amount of weight?
Like the old saying says:
You can never go home again.
And that means that
You can never recapture or regain your youth.
I'm overweight.
Not by much.
But by society's standards, I'm probably fat.
I have to stop being ashamed of myself.
Along with making silly excuses about why I am fat.
As well as putting an end to the false promises
That I make to myself about losing my weight.
Drastic weight loss will not happen overnight.
I didn't gain the excess weight overnight,
So I can't expect to lose it overnight.
I have to try and make the effort
Not to gain any more weight.
But,what I have gained
Is probably here to stay.
So I'd better get used to the way I look.
Because, that's me, baby.
I need to enjoy the time that I have left to live
And start living life to the fullest.
If someone looks upon me with disdain,
So what?
It's their problem, not mine.
And if it does become my problem,
I will solve it the quickest way possible.
My life up until now has been pretty good.
And if gaining a few extra pounds
Is the price I have to pay for it,
Then so be it.

I Am...

...getting married.
Again, for the first time!
I've been married before,
But there was no union in that marriage.
There was plenty of union before the marriage,
So much so that we had to get married.
But once I said "I do",
She said, "not very often".
But, enough about my previous marriage.
It was a disaster.
It is forever dead to me,
And will stay buried.
I'm not sure how long I've been divorced,
But, I know I've been separated and divorced
Going on fifteen years.
Fifteen years of being alone was horrible.
The only thing worse than being alone
Is being with someone you can't stand.
Hence, the reason for the divorce.
This time things will be different.
This time we will share our worlds with each other.
So, if there is an argument;
One can't hide in their own world,
Because that world is really our world now.
For, we are one in all forms and manner.
There is no longer a me or an I,
But an us and we.
We come together to form this union
Long before we are married.
There is perfect symmetry between us.
We are as opposite as night and day,
But we all know that opposites attract.
We also know it takes two to make a marriage,
And we are the two that will make this marriage succeed.
It also takes two to break a marriage.
My first wife and her mom did a damn good job in my first marriage.
But I've learned, and those lessons will not be repeated!

I Am...

...God.
And it kills me that all some people can just speak for me.
And, supposedly in my own words.
But why is it, that only the ones who "speak" for me,
Profit from me?
I see that I am still the best way to make a buck.
Look at the people who wrote the Left Behind series.
How will this writing convert followers to my name?
It won't.
It will just pad the pockets of those who really don't care about me.
Those who feed off the guilt and fear of people
Who DO believe in me.
Please know that I am not a Capitalist.
I never have been, and never will be.
I am very much the socialist.
Because I want everyone to share in my kingdom,
No matter what their ethnic, social or financial status might be.
There is more than enough for everyone, to go around.
There is no excuse for anyone to go hungry,
Or to be without clothes and shelter.
People make war in my name,
Killing countless numbers of my children.
People make love in my name,
Chanting my name over and over as they fertilize the seed of life.
It's almost as if
You go kill your brother,
As you create his replacement.
What's up with you people?
Don't you have a clue to what I'm all about?
It's not about spreading my name through death and destruction.
Nor is it moaning my name through primal, carnal acts of lust and love.
It's not about making people feel guilty,
Just because they don't visibly believe in me.
I'm the only one who knows
What is in someone's mind, heart, and soul.
And believe me when I say this:
Almost everyone in creation believes in me
In some form or fashion.
It just might not be your form or fashion.
I've had thousands of names,
From Creator to Zeus.
I am all those gods you read about in mythology.

Even the supposed non-believers, do believe in me.
They are just making their own reward
By stating that they don't.
What gets to me the most,
That gives me the biggest regret I have in humanity,
Is when people choose to hate in my name.
I am not about hatred of any kind.
I love all of my children.
I want no holy war or righteous crusade done in my name.
Because no one profits from genocide,
Except for those, who manipulate truly weak people in my name.
I don't care if you are black, blue, green, or purple,
Or if you wear a dress or pants,
Have a beard or shave your legs,
Or are heterosexual or homosexual,
As long as you don't impose your will upon someone else,
(For your own monetary and personal gain)
And you live your life to the fullest extent possible.
I love you and welcome you into my realm.
Love is what I'm all about.
Love, not in the carnal sense,
But in the spiritual sense.
Loving is so much easier that hating.
Try it sometime.
Try loving your enemies rather than hating them.
You'll find it's the easier road to travel.

I Am...

...going nowhere.
At supersonic speed.
I live under a wide spectrum of fear:
Ranging from not being a true daughter to my mom
To giving up on my children, everyday it seems.
I can't seem to win, because I keep making the same mistakes
Over and over again.
It would be okay if it really was the same mistake,
But I keep a plethora of mistakes on hand to use at any time.
Always ready to give me yet another setback.
My best friend says that I should star in a reality TV show about my life.
Call it "AMERICAN TRASH",
Because America loves its trash.
I laugh at him and shake my head in disbelief.
Almost anyone, except maybe a Jerry Springer guest,
Would be highly insulted by such an innuendo.
I know I'm not trashy in the least, but like the Good Book says;
Trash begets trash.
And I do seem to do my share of begetting nowadays.
I've always been unlucky in love:
From a mother who adopted me,
And calls me her adopted daughter,
(Like she doesn't want to get blamed for bringing me into this world)
To every man I have ever gotten to know on an intimate basis.
Using me for their own purposes,
No matter how sick and demented that might have been.
Even my best friend used me just to get his kicks.
I was so starved for attention and wanting to feel needed,
I was such a willing victim.
Then he went and did something really crazy.
He married someone else.
Somebody who won't or can't do
All the things that a woman, as hungry for love as I am, is willing to do.
How dare him!
And then he has the nerve to preach to me,
That I should be more selective about whom I date.
Of all the nerve!
He didn't seem to mind that I wasn't selective about him.
Now that he is gone and I should wait around being lonely?
For who? Him to get divorced?
Even if he does, he is way too expensive for me to keep.
He does try to help me, by giving out free advice.

But that doesn't make me feel alive the way that I do
When I'm at the mercy of a lover.
Since I could never please anyone as I was growing up,
I'm trying to please as many as I can, now that I'm all grown up.
We all have to die of something. People who smoke die of cancer.
My new boyfriend is an old boyfriend
Who I met on the rebound from my best friend.
He's black and I'm white. My mom says that I'm betraying my race.
Whatever. He wants me.
He's good looking, great in bed, and he keeps coming back to me.
He even got another white girl pregnant, just a month ago.
But, he didn't want to leave me to be with her.
He even went so far as suggesting that he and she
Move in with me and my two teenage sons.
How dare him use me like that!
But now, he has left this pregnant woman to be with me.
Am I proud?
"Sucks to be her", is what I say.
Sure, he did a stupid thing
By selling drugs to an undercover cop.
But we all make mistakes.
I know my sons won't make THAT mistake.
They know that drugs are bad.
My best friend asks me,
What kind of message I am sending to my boys?
My boyfriend doesn't own a car,
So I drive him back and forth to work, when he has a job.
I pay for his food and buy him clothes and
He even shares his other women with me.
My best friend asks me jokingly if, my mom knows that I'm a lesbian.
You know,
I used to be worried about my best friend being high maintenance.
And I think that I took the cheap way out.
And bottom line:
I know that I am making someone happy.
My boyfriend needs me and I know he wants me.
Why else would he keep coming back to me?
What is everyone missing here?
He loves me!
Why can't anyone be happy for me?

I Am...

...in Heaven.
And believe me when I say that
It doesn't get any better than this.
How can this be true you ask?
How could I have achieved my eternal reward
And still be counted among the living?
Heaven is not really an eternal reward.
Like Jesus said;
"The Kingdom of Heaven is at hand."
At hand.
Do you know what that means?
It means presently,
Or here and now.
It does not mean, thousands of years into the future.
Jesus never told us we would go to Heaven.
He did say
We will go to be with the Father.
His Father,
Your Father,
My Father,
Our Father,
He's all the same person.
When we die,
We go to be with our Father.
We don't go to Heaven,
Because Heaven is for the living.
Being with the Father, is when we have passed from this mortal plane.
You've probably been to Heaven countless times
And been unaware of it.
I realized it just a few weeks ago
When I was lying on my waterbed
With my wife and two daughters.
Heaven can't be better than this.
Who cares about streets paved with gold,
When your loved ones are around you?
When I make love to my wife,
I'm in Heaven.
How can pearly gates compare to that?
Where is Jesus right now?
Most people would say in their heart or soul.
Or, He's with God,
Or maybe He's in heaven.

It states in the Bible when two or three are gathered in His name,
He am there.
Maybe we are there as well.
Gathered together in love:
Love of God,
Love of yourself,
And love of your loved ones.
Because there is no desire in Heaven
Except to love as much as possible.
Most people would have to see Heaven to believe in it.
But really,
All you have to do
Is to believe in it
To see Heaven.

I Am...

...in Hell.
Just like you are,
And just like everyone else is, as well.
Hell, like Heaven, is for the living, not the unsavory dead.
My wife and I have argued about my concept of Hell
Since the time we first met.
She came up with the perfect definition of Hell:
The eternal separation from God.
BINGO!!!
Where we differ, though,
Is that I don't believe in the company line of fire and brimstone.
No one is whaling or gnashing to having a thirst unquenched.
There is no demonic overlord of Hell.
There is only you.
You are that demonic overlord of Hell.
Because the Hell that you are in, is your own personal Hell.
And no one else's.
If you share your Hell with someone,
It's because you've invited them into your Hell.
Lucky them.
With a friend or lover like you, who needs enemies?
Want me to describe Hell to you?
Hell is anything you do that separates you from God.
Think of all the things you do that separate you from God.
Are you connected to God when you go to Wal-mart?
Or when you go to the restroom?
Yes I'm picking extremely mundane examples,
But, is the brain freeze beginning to thaw?
From a meaningless sexual encounter,
To a meaningless conversation on the phone,
It's all Hell,
If you are not connected with God, in all that you do.
Once you become connected to God you are back in Heaven.
When you choose to disconnect you go back to being in Hell.
It just one or the other.
Because, there is no Purgatory here, folks.
So you decide where you want to spend your time:
Heaven or Hell.
The choice is yours.

I Am...

...interlocked & intertwined.
With my heart and soul.
Because, my one true love is by my side.
I know that everything is just perfect,
As we lay underneath the stars
On a warm silent night,
With our arms wrapped around each other.
I feel your passion thaw my emotions
As you make me fell protected.
Holding and kissing me so gently,
As our shadows dance a dance of love,
Underneath the moonlit sky.
We don't want to break the silence of the night,
So we kiss the words we want to say.
At times our kisses are so delicately sweet.
At other times it seems that
We are on a battlefield making war, not love.
We melt into each other as the fervor of our lust reaches its crescendo.
The wind carries our moans somewhere into space.
We break the silence by telling each other that
There is no place we would rather be,
Than to be right here,
Right now,
With each other.
Our arms and legs interlocked,
As our souls are intertwined into each other,
Under the moonlit sky.
As of right this moment,
Heaven is on earth.

I Am...

...Judas,
But this time not just of Iscariot.
This time,
I am the Judas of your soul.
That's right.
There is a Judas in all of us.
But, before we deal with the Judas that we all love to hate,
Let's deal with the Judas within each of us.
This poem will be the real story of Judas,
And all will know the truth behind the legend of Judas.
Am I the Jewish Benedict Arnold?
Not hardly.
And no,
I did not become Count Vladimir Dracula either
(Like the movie portrays).
I appear in many places in the Bible.
I once soothed Hagar about her baby,
I told Lot to leave Sodom,
I even wrestled Jacob all night as a rite of passage for him.
I comforted Daniel in the lion's den,
I was countless other places, as well.
Each time,
I do the will of God, without question.
The only time that I was not known,
Was when I took on the appearance of Judas.
Jesus Christ himself did not recognize me.
But Jesus was only a human,
Even though he was The Christ.
He was troubled by the weariness of his journeys,
And the weight of his impending sacrifice.
His disciples did not know me,
Because they were worried about their own lives.
That's why many weren't present at the crucifixion.
They were all looking out for number one.
I was supposed to be a herald of a new age.
That's why Jesus said,
"Woe is the man who betrays me,
He will wish he was never born."
I was NEVER born,
I was created,
As were my brothers and sisters
To do the work of God.

No matter what His wishes,
We are there to accomplish the task.
Even if that task is to build a rock that's too heavy to be picked up.
I am an Angel of the Lord.
And it was my task to betray the Christ into the hands of the enemy.
An unenviable task and I knew that I would be hated
From the moment it happened.
But it had to happen.
And I was chosen to make it happen.
Why is it said that I hung myself?
In today's world,
That would be an act of cowardice.
But in the world that I come from,
It showed an attempt at regaining honor.
Obviously,
I did not hang myself.
For, I cannot die.
The story of me hanging myself
Was told to those writing the testaments
Through their dreams, to show that I was redeeming myself.
Do you not see any parallels in this story and in your life?
Do we not betray our loved ones
Countless times over.
And then try to redeem ourselves
By literally or figuratively killing ourselves,
In the hopes of regaining our lost honor?
Today's customs are not the same as they were
Two thousand years ago.
Only in the Orient,
Is there any hope of reclaiming your honor by suicide.
So you see,
It's not what I did,
That was so wrong in the eyes of man.
It was how my actions were perceived
By those who don't know the whole story.
And now you know the truth.
Not only about the historical Judas,
But, about the Judas who resides within each of us.

I Am...

...just a whisper.
I can be your greatest temptation.
O.K.
I can also be your most mild temptation, as well.
I'm what you want to hear, as well as, what you want to read.
I can be so sneaky, that at first,
You probably won't even know I'm manipulating you to my will.
Want an example?
Say you are a woman, attractive enough to be sexy,
But need to lose a few pounds first.
You are 36-ish and at your sexual peak,
Except that, you just aren't peaking with your current partner,
Who happens to be your husband.
Yes you're married.
For the second time, I might add.
You have two children, a dog, a good job, and a nice house.
Sounds like the American Dream, doesn't it?
Do you not realize how lucky and blessed you are?
But your house can't be a home anymore, because of me.
I mean, all of your friends want what you are giving up.
Duh!
Think of the security that you have, both at work and at home.
Your sons think that you are really cool.
But hey. They're just another statistic, now.
Your husband used to feel so lucky to have you.
He doesn't have too many bad habits.
He's not a druggie or a drinker, and he doesn't beat you.
But he does take you for granted, as most husbands will do.
Did you not learn that from the first time you were married?
It's a two way street, and all that you have to do,
is to make a concerted effort
To have as much fun as you did while you were dating each other,
Before you got married.
Think of all the sacrifices that you would make, just to see each other,
To kiss each other, to be lovers, to be each others escape?
It used to be so much fun. Didn't it?
Not so much fun anymore, though. Is it?
You think you are in a rut. Don't you?
You miss all the action, excitement, and the constant vibe of being....
You fill in the blank.
You don't have the freedom that your friends do.
Your friends talk about all the fun that they have

And good times galore.
But what they really want is,
All the things that you are so casually giving up,
Just so you can be like your friends.
Look at your friends, who you envy so much.
Look at the lives they took for granted.
Do you see what is missing in their life?
Why follow in their footsteps?
Do you think you could really beat the odds?
Why do you think that
You can find happiness some place other than home?
But then, you can never go home again.
Can you?
So, why would you want to be with other unhappy people?
Don't you know, that any of your so-called friends
Would end their friendship with you
For just a chance at the happiness that you have had?
And you want to flush it all away, as fast as possible?
Why would you do that?
Oh I know. Because of me.
Don't you see I slithered into your life and whispered to you
All the things that you think you want in life?
Do you know my real name?
Like the song states,
Say my name.
Say my name.
And no.
I am not Satan.
There is no such being.
Your limited mind is just trying to find an easy answer.
My true name is free will.
The zealots will disagree.
Because they need to have a fall guy.
And what better guy than some mythical creature?
I am the same free will that you traded paradise for in Eden.
I am your free will.
And you just keep making the wrong choices.
Love is sacrifice.
What part of that don't you understand?

At least you will be as miserable, as your family and friends,
(Who are supporting you in this mistake) will be.
But then,
We all know, that misery loves company,
So.
You might be happy.
But,
I bet you won't be.
Especially, after you see all that you have given up.
And for what?
A chance to recapture some part of your youth?
It wasn't worth having then.
And that goes doubly, now.

I Am...

...just sitting here.
I'm minding my own business, without a worry in the world.
And then it happens.
Everything in my world goes completely white.
It's as if God dropped a ton of white stuff on me.
Am I dreaming?
I know I'm awake, because I can hear myself scream.
I'm not cold, so it can't be snow.
That's when I hear this thumping, swiping sound.
It starts out dull, but then, gets louder and louder,
As if it's coming for me.
Then nothing.
The white stuff is gone,
Only to be replaced by complete darkness.
`I'm not sure where I am, but I do know, that I'm not happy to be here.
I can't seem to move: am I tied up?
I hear the cry of a small child near me:
What is going on?
What is that ungodly hiss?
The louder the hiss gets, the louder the baby screams.
Sounds like steam, but I'm not getting any warmer,
Or wetter, in my dark surroundings.
But the hiss now sounds like a jet engine.
Am I at the airport?
Where am I going?
I can't remember,
If only I could see.
Where are you, baby?
I feel like I can almost touch your scream:
Where are you baby?
I cry out in an anguished moan.
Then all of a sudden there is light and a tapping on the window.
"That'll be six dollars for the car wash, mister."
My Daddy turns around and asks me and my baby sister,
"Wasn't that fun?"
The agony of being three,
And going through the car wash,
For the very first time.

Inspired by my beautiful Daughter, Kelleigh-Jaymes

I Am...

...like clockwork.
Because it happens at the same time,
Same place,
Every night,
Just like clockwork.
You're there,
Humming some insane nursery rhyme:
Mommy is there,
Humming some insane nursery rhyme:
Sissy is there,
Humming some insane nursery rhyme:
I'm there.
And THEY are there, as well.
I'm screaming bloody murder.
Tears are rolling down my cheeks.
I'm so upset,
But everyone is looking at the TV.
Can't anyone else see THEM?
I even close my eyes, but THEY are still around me.
Is this some sick joke?
What is wrong with you people?
I scream, and all you do, is offer me a drink.
Am I the only one who's aware of what's happening here?
I'm not thirsty.
I just want you to protect me,
To keep THEM away from me,
From MOMMY,
From Sissy,
And even from you.
The anguish I feel,
Daaa HORRWWAW!
Has everyone been drugged?
I take the drink,
Not thinking, that it might be tainted,
By whatever is affecting my family.
I gulp it down, like it will be my last.
I'm hoping that it will calm me.
Boy! You mix one mean drink.
It has the desired effect upon me.
It relaxes me.
My body becomes totally warm and fuzzy,
My mind is in a trance, and

I feel as if I'm being cast out to sea.
My ship is rolling with the waves,
As wave after wave after wave,
Keeps rocking me further out to sea.
I'm just drifting away.
Then, all of a sudden,
I'm back in my living room.
But, THEY are back, as well.
Deadlier then before, and
In all different shapes and sizes.
I'm screaming my throat raw.
I think I wet my pants.
I'm so distraught.
Why doesn't someone do something?
I fling my unfinished drink to the floor.
I'm crying to the heavens above,
Hoping that I will wake up everyone else in the room.
But to no avail.
Everyone continues to laugh and talk,
As is if I'm not even there.
What is wrong with these people?
Don't they realize the danger?
Then someone stands up and starts to look for something.
A formula they say.
For a new, nasty weapon, maybe?
Now I'll show them who they're dealing with.
Wait! That's not a weapon!
It's a dry diaper and some pajamas.
They pick my bottle of formula up, off the floor.
Oooohhh,
The agonies of being eighteen months old,
And fighting being put to sleep each night.

Inspired by my beautiful Daughter, Bridgette.

I Am...

*** this poem contains adult situations***

...living the Horror.
I have been, ever since I started my period,
At the age of eleven.
He claimed that he knew my mind.
He boasted that he knew my heart.
He bragged about knowing what makes me tick.
How he could get such a rise
From my young, tender body.
He has nicotine-stained trembling hands,
Rancid putrid breath.
He reeks of Jack Daniel's and cheap cigars.
Is this how all girls learn to love?
Never knowing when he will come for me again.
He proudly states that he is making me into a woman.
I am now a woman,
At least forty times over.
Some girls at sixteen
Have never been kissed.
At thirteen,
I am just the object
Of a madman's lust.
He is at least three times my age.
Over and over and over.
Every night, when Mother is away,
Working to pay all the bills, because he refuses to.
Since I'm living in hell,
Do I ask Satan to release me?
With my innocence forever corrupted,
I wander aimlessly
With no path to follow.
Just to find that my dreams are all hollow.
What could I have done differently?
Maybe, I should have been born a boy.
My cries and pleas go unanswered.
The police,
With more important doughnuts to eat,
Tell me that I should mind my father.
My leering minister tells me, that
The Bible teaches me to respect my father.
My father tells me

That I must submit to him,
Or, he will show me how.
I have no one to love,
But everyone to hate.
Is this what love is all about?
The anger that grows inside of me
Will only seal my fate.
Perhaps it is a fact:
People just don't care.
Can death be all that bad?
Pop some pills:
No more pain-
Just one step over the line:
No more pain.
And, no more hopes or dreams.
I haven't had those for a long time, anyway.
But, no more pain.
That sounds so good.
Let's see how much pleasure he'll receive,
When he's having sex with my lifeless corpse!

Please... If you find yourself or know of someone in this
kind of situation, please get help. Go to child services or the
police. The police are the good guys: they will help. Do not
let something like this continue and ruin more lives. These
sick bastards need to be put away for a very long time.

I Am...

...my own worst enemy.
I could be the richest man that there is.
But, I make the poorest decisions possible.
I bitch about being alone,
But I neglect the people in my life.
I whine about not being married,
But all I want is a divorce, once I am married.
I complain about not finding a job,
But complain louder about the work
When I do have a job.
I go out to spread the gospel,
But then come home,
And commit all types of atrocities in my heart.
I slowly move toward my own goal,
But move like greased lightning,
To stop someone else from reaching theirs.
I pray and preach,
But betray God at every turn.
I'm your truest friend to your face,
But your sworn enemy behind your back.
What is wrong with me?
Nothing,
Not one thing.
I'm as flawed as you,
And these things are what make us so.

I Am...

...not about.
Just as our love is not about
The gifts that have been bestowed upon us;
Our love is not about the places where we have traveled.
Our love is not about your old lovers,
Nor is our love about any of my ex-lovers.
Our love is not about paying any of your bills,
Just like our love is just not about you.

Our love is about us.

Us
Who will be there for each other,
No matter what adversities may arise.
For better or for worse,
For richer or for poorer,
Until death do us part.
Us
Who receives more joy in giving than getting.
And Us
Who are the better part of ourselves.

Ourselves
Who are bonded with each other:
Not just through some carnal primal intimate dance.
Ourselves
Who know that better days lie ahead.
That fulfillment of our dreams is just a sweet "I DO" away.
I love you on all planes,
Spiritually, mentally, physically, and emotionally.
Too bad that you can't get past "not about".

I Am...

...not God.
God is me,
Me is God,
But I am not God.
Sound confusing?
If God is me does that not make me God?
Not exactly.
You see, where God is all of me: I am just a tiny part of God.
Just like you are a part of God, and everyone who has ever lived is.
Do you want to see a picture of God?
Place everyone in a mosaic together,
The believers and the non-believers; and that's what God looks like.
God needs each little piece of us to stay whole.
When one of us dies, that gives God a gray hair.
Or, when someone is murdered or raped,
That is a scar upon the body of God.
And we all know some scars penetrate into our very soul.
The same can be said about God's scars.
We all make up the body of God.
But being a tiny piece of God plays a very important role.
God needs us just as much as we need God.
God needs for us to believe in Him,
Because if we don't, He will cease to exist.
And if that happens, we will also cease to exist, the nanosecond after.
Do you see how everyone makes up the body of God?
If one part of the body
Fails to believe in the other part, it matters not the least.
The unbelieving part is still a part of the whole body.
Take me for example-
Because of a car accident back in 1989, the left side of my body
Can't do the same things as the right side of my body.
But do I ignore my left side or pretend that it's not there?
No,
Because the left side of my body is still part of my body.
And, I don't want to lose my left side:
Just like God does not want to lose sight of a non-believer.
So remember how this poem started...
God is me,
And me is God,
But I am not God.

I Am...

...NOT proud to be an American.
I bet our founding fathers
Would hang their heads in shame.
America is at war,
Funded by American tax dollars,
Not for some justifiable reason;
But for the one thing
That we as a nation
Worship above all else,
(Even above God and life itself).
I'm talking about the almighty dollar.
Do you realize,
That with the money we have spent,
Or maybe borrowed from China,
Every American Tax payer,
(You, me, your family, your co-workers)
Everyone in America
Could have had a million dollars instead?
Now, I don't know about you,
But I'd rather have a million dollars
Than having our sons & daughters die
In some God forsaken country.
America's leaders rant and rave,
Quite calmly I might add,
About the human rights that are being abused,
And the need to eliminate a threat,
Not only to America,
But also to our allies.
And America's leaders are willing to make the ultimate sacrifice:
And send someone else's sons and daughters,
To some God forsaken foreign land.
Where they will supposedly eliminate the threat to us,
And liberate the people of Iraq
(Whether they want to be liberated or not).
Our leaders tell us that human rights are being violated
On a daily basis over there,
And that weapons of mass destruction,
Along with all sorts of chemical weapons,
Are being stockpiled somewhere in Iraq.

And we need to make sure, that those weapons
Do not fall into the hands of terrorists.
But, since this war has started,
No chemical weapons
Or weapons of mass destruction have been found.
At least we are stopping the human rights violations,
Even though this war is being funded by human rights violations
That occur in America
Thousands of times on a daily basis.
Of course,
The leaders of America
Turn a blind eye,
And a deaf ear,
To these human rights violations.
How can this be possible you ask?
One word explains it all.
ABORTION,
The ultimate human rights violation
Where we kill babies at our own discretion.
America aborts more babies in one day,
Than our enemies violate human rights in a month.
How can the leaders of America
Ignore the fact,
That abortion is a clear violation of human rights?
The all-mighty dollar strikes again.
Or in this case,
The all-mighty TAX dollar.
Every time a child is aborted,
The government gets their blood money.

So,
Go support the war effort.
Be a proud American,
And abort a baby today.

It's for a good cause.

I Am...

...passion.
And just like the song states,
Some people live and die for passion.
Everything has an opposite;
Except for me.
Love has Hate,
Good has Bad,
And Light has Dark.
But for these things to be complete,
There needs to be a passion about them.
There needs to be me,
To make everything complete.
I reside within every being,
And it is only through self-control,
That I might be tamed.
Everything one does,
Reflects on the passions in their life.
The movies one watches,
The music one dances to,
The books one reads,
The candidates one votes for,
Even the food that one eats;
Show the personal passions of that person.
Complete is a very good word to describe passion,
Because passion is the
Alpha and Omega of emotions.
You have to be passionate about something,
And once you are, it becomes complete.
There are different passions depending upon your age,
Especially when you're asleep.
When you are young, you dream very passionately
Of the things that you want to do and accomplish in life.
A child dreams of being
A space ranger,
A super spy,
Or their favorite super-hero.
An older person dreams of things that could have been,
Or remembers things that were, both bad and good.

A middle-aged person
Dreams the best and worst of both worlds:
All are very exciting dreams.
Does anyone ever dream a boring dream?
You can dream that you are
The World Champion Heavy Weight Boxer,
A super spy,
Or back in the arms of a long, lost love.
People dream of every would've, could've,
And should've beens in their life.
There are no unanswered questions
Or regrets in anyone's dreams.
People can recapture both time and space in their dreams,
Because nothing is sacred in their dreams.
Everything is always wide-open and full speed ahead.
No psyche or emotional barrier
Can withstand a dream onslaught.
All dreams are full of passion,
Because the dreamer's life is completely full of passion.
If there was another word out there that is the opposite of passion,
I'm not sure what it would be.
Passion lies deep within everyone:
It is the very core of the soul.
Passion is just as deadly as an atomic bomb at ground zero,
And can be the greatest force on Earth.
Control one's passion,
And you literally can control the world.

I Am...

...perfect.
But perfection does not make me divine.
Divinity is being without sin.
So you see,
Perfection does not mean to be without sin.
It means perfection through and through.
I have fallen from grace over and over again,
But that has not stopped me from attaining perfection.
"How can this be?" you ask.
Aren't we taught that we come into this world as a sinner?
Yes.
But this teaching is wrong.
Perfection is an ability, or better yet,
A state of being that we are born into.
That's right.
I'm saying that we are all born as perfect specimens of God.
The fall from grace comes when we learn how to sin.
Everything outside of love is taught to us.
But learning how to sin
Does not prevent us from being perfect.
And I'm not talking about being a perfect sinner.
But then again... maybe I am.
Because there is one thing that is as certain as death and taxes:
We, meaning humanity as a whole, will not stop sinning.
But, as easily as we choose to sin we can choose to be perfect.
It's just that simple.
We just need to learn how to regain our perfect nature.
You see,
Perfection is the first of many gifts that God grants to us
As we are being born into this world.
We just choose not to be perfect,
Thus spurning this bountiful and precious gift from God.
WARNING!!
Be very wary of the so-called fundamentalists
Who preach that we are born sinners.
And can never be anything else,
Unless we follow their teachings and of course give them lots of money.
All in the name of God of course.
But like the Bible states,
These people will get their own reward.
And, I guarantee you that God knows them not.
The problem with this sort of people, other than their greed,

And lust for power and control,
Is that they don't see the big picture.
They have tunnel vision or blinders on.
They can't see the forest for the trees.
There are worlds within worlds,
And there is perfection within all these worlds.
Take a raindrop, for example:
Each raindrop is a world within our world.
We know there are things alive in these worlds.
We just have not been able to communicate with these creatures yet.
Perfection is all around us.
We just choose to ignore it.
Want to see perfection in the world we live in?
Look at the animal kingdom or the insect or plant kingdom,
Or even life under the sea.
Only man, be it male or female, fell from grace.
Only man.
All these other worlds and kingdoms are still perfect.
They never fell from grace.
We have to make a choice to learn from their example.
We could if we just took the time, and
We would see perfection in our world as well.
Even though I have fallen from grace countless times,
I have actually attained perfection a few times.
An example, of attaining perfection, is the love I have for my wife.
I no longer have the wanderlust for life.
Even though I still enjoy being center stage on the mike,
I no longer have that craving to be noticed by all.
All, meaning every woman in the surrounding area.
The love that I have for my children is perfect,
And my effort at being a step-father is perfect, as well.
The meals that I cook are beyond perfection!
But, let's not lose focus.
As long as our motives and intentions are pure,
We can attain perfection.
But, the minute we put our wants, needs, and desires
Into the equation, it all goes askew.
If I can attain perfection, then you should have no problem doing so.

I Am...

...faster than a speeding bullet: is this a man?
More Powerful than a locomotive: is this a man?
Able to leap tall buildings in a single bound: is this a man?
Pushing out 8 pounds of life between my legs: is this a man?

Behind every great man is a woman,   Pulling his strings.
Men are full of boasts,   bluster,   and frontier gibberish.
But a woman's silence is...   The ultimate weapon of power.

Look up in the sky!   It's a bird, it's a plane, it's a man!
Are men really   stronger,   faster,   or smarter, than women?

Men have to prove their worth.
But a woman just gives her approval.

Women don't have penis envy: Men do, every inch of the way.

The first three lines of this poem   are pure fantasy.
Where as the fourth line   is pure reality.

There is no such thing as a

Super-Man.

But look about you:
Wonder Woman is all around.

Let's face it,

Men
          meet us,
                    do us,
                              and then are done with us.
But every woman has the one thing most men want,
                    And don't be such a man and ask what.

Men fall from grace over and over again,
                    But women are perfectly, imperfect.

I Am...

...pregnant.
I have a life forming within me!
Is this how Eve felt?
I am the mother of a whole new world.
It is so wonderfully horrible:
The excitement of being pregnant
Is as great as
The fear of being pregnant.
I have to change my whole life-style.
I can't smoke or drink anymore,
Nor can I do any heavy anti-psychotic drugs.
Not that I would do any of those things anyway.
I have to make sure that this baby will be healthy.
I have to take care of this baby;
I just hope there is someone to take care of me.
I know he will try,
He is a man of perfect intentions,
But the only thing perfect about him is his intentions.
At least I don't have to worry about my man not finding me attractive.
I know he loves me,
And will always be by my side,
In sickness and in health,
For better or for worse,
Until death do us part.
I really don't think even death will keep us apart, for long.
This is not the first time I've been pregnant.
Really it should be old hat to me by now.
But each time has been totally different.
The discomfort is different, as well as, the new type of pain
That accompanies each pregnancy.
Maybe I had morning sickness during my first pregnancy,
But now it should be called the 24/7 sickness.
I had chili–dog cravings the first time around.
My only craving this time, is to have this baby as soon as possible.
Do we want a boy or a girl?
It doesn't matter because this baby will be loved,
By two of the luckiest parents in the world.

I Am...

...regretful.
All the should'ves, could'ves, and would'ves come back to haunt me.
The music drones on.
With it comes all the laughter, clatter, and chatter of the party.
Only we are not distracted by the ensuing chaos.
No matter how close we might be, we are still worlds apart.
Even though WE are no longer a couple,
WE will forever be linked to each other.
All I see is her, all she sees is me, and I know we are connected.
But we aren't alone, WE are never alone, no matter who we're with.
But we still share our special moments together.
Her scent and smiles invade my mind and soul.
The special look she gives me, reads me like a book.
The trials and tribulations we have both endured will end tonight,
As my ravaged heart has now been made whole again.
I must have her; I must take her back.
I have to at least tell her to release this burden I carry.
Time has healed all my wounds.
But, no matter how much time has passed,
All my feelings for her, have remained the same.
The time is now for me to act upon my passion.
I must act. No guts no glory. Is she as scared as I am?
I'm shaking now as I force myself through the throng that blocks me,
As my date, unknowing of the battle raging within me, follows.
Sweating now,
I breathe deep and try to stay calm and in focus – stay sane.
Trembling now, I want to express my love to her,
Along with all my hopes and desires,
Which she knows, oh, so intimately.
Weeping now, I shuffle away into my date's arms.
Sobbing forever, as I leave behind the woman of my dreams,
Who is so right for me,
To be with a woman, who is so wrong for me.
I'm such a coward. The music continues to drone on,
Haunting me with all the would'ves, could'ves, and should'ves.

I Am...

...remembering.
Being six, I think.
This particular day was just beautiful.
Mom was in a good mood,
Breakfast was really good this morning,
And I even got to see the early morning cartoons
Instead of the news program.
Mom tells me that we will even eat at McDonalds.
Wow, McDonalds!
Thanks Mom.
After the doctors visit, she continues.
WWWWWHHHHHAAAAATTTTTT????!!!!????
Doctors Visit?!?
And, as if on cue,
The water works begin.
And I cry as I never have before.
The Devil and the fiery pits of Hell
Pale in comparison to the agonies of the Doctor!
The Grinch who Stole Christmas
Is nothing compared to the Doctor!
The most fearful Haunted House,
Is like a sand castle in high tide, next to the Doctor.
Oh the humanity!
Mom holds my hand as we enter the office.
After a short wait in the lobby,
During which, Mom tells me a story to keep me calm,
We are ushered into a room that reeks of alcohol.
I ask to be excused to go to the bathroom,
And I am allowed to go down the hall.
I instead, sneak into another room and hide underneath the table.
I am finally found and after a quick check-up,
I'm told I will need two shots in my derriere.
If I could cuss,
I'd scream, "Hell no, lady!"
I fight to fend off the doctor,
Wishing I had a gun.
It would be self-defense.
Any court of my peers would find me innocent.
No matter how I scramble,
Or how I duck,
I am finally trapped in the corner by two orderlies.
I scream bloody murder as I receive the first shot:

Which the nurse tells me will not hurt.
Why do they lie to me?
I get into trouble when I lie,
But my Mom says nothing about the nurse's lies.
The second shot hits home.
All the while the nurse is smiling, her evil smile.
And she's telling me "That didn't hurt a bit now, did it?"
If I knew the words that I know now,
I'd say,
"Hell yeah, lady"
"Let me shove two needles in your ass and see how you like it."
But I can't.
And I don't say anything.
I'm only six.
So I rub my butt and begin to think of those McDonald French Fries.

Yummy, yummy, yummy!!

I Am...

...Satan.
And I don't exist, except in your heart and soul.
Some people believe that I am plotting the downfall
And subjugation of mankind.
That's your job, not mine.
You are your own worst enemy, not me.
Not one person on this planet can prove that I exist.
Not one thing happens in daily life that says,
This is the work of the Devil.
Sure, it might be evil, but it is the evil stench of man
Who commits all types of atrocities, not me.
I'm innocent of any wrong-doing.
But, supposedly true born-again believers have faith that I exist.
In fact,
They have more faith in the things I couldn't do, even if I did exist,
Than they have in God, who does exist.
I'm supposedly a fallen angel or the creator of the Anti-Christ:
But, I'm none of those things.
What I am, is a figment, pure and simple, of your imagination.
Thousands of years ago the Hebrew people were just starting out.
Back then, everyone had a god.
The Hebrews had to create their own heroes and myths
To compete with those of other cultures.
That's how the faith spread, back in those days,
Through myth and lore.
I didn't even come about from the ancient Hebrews.
Abraham and Moses never even knew that I existed.
I was adopted, you could say, into the Hebrew lore.
I had my own little following, until Joshua went on a rampage
Throughout the Middle East.
My story was adopted into the Hebrew Myths
Through some guy named Job, who wasn't even Jewish.
You keep me alive through your belief in me.
I have no power over you,
Except, that which you allow me to have, which can be quite a bit.

Thanks buddy.

I Am...

...silently hoping.
Hoping that this poem
Will rekindle your future, by just tasting the past.
I hope with all my being, that you get that frothy feeling of love,
As you see your parents revel
In their chaotic, tumultuous, throes of love.
Let it be known that I coveted your mother,
And wanted her from the moment I laid eyes on her.
Until death do us part, or until we're too old to care,
In about eighty-three years, I think.
Once, we two were very modern, for our time.
Now the cobblestones of our memories are being trafficked
By the latest, congested snapshots of love.
Today's couples move at the full speed of anxiety,
Becoming tainted by the false reality of non-commitment.
As they calmly sip their mocha cappuccinos,
They do little to extinguish the eternal flames of fear.
Beware!
Because, this fear is contagious, having created false illusions.
So,
Stand up to your fear, and it will be feared no longer.
Take a chance and grasp hold of life with all that you love,
As tightly as you can.
Never, ever let go.
Because, if you do, your snapshot of love
Will never be made into a feature film
Starring you and your love,
Just like your mom and I had.
It is time for you to take the lead role, and hopefully your movie
Will last as long and have as many sequels as our movie has.

I Am...

...standing naked,
Before a world
That pays me no heed,
Since I wear the guilt and constraints of society.
I am all alone in a world of millions.
I scream, yet no one hears,
Because they are too busy screaming, as well.
For what?
Maybe for the innocence that has long been lost.
My innocence has long been shattered.
It was tempted away from me:
The way that Adam was tempted with that apple.
Like Adam, I traded my innocence for knowledge.
A knowledge that gave me no power and a case of crabs
That humiliated me to no end.
Society can fit you like a glove,
And those were the first two pieces of clothing
That put me on the fast track into society.
Unlike now, I used to be sociably acceptable.
I was a mover, a shaker, and a part of the me generation.
I was a person on the way up,
All the while not knowing that, I was about to hit rock bottom.
And when I did hit bottom, I didn't just go splat;
I think I bounced a few dozen times on the hard pavement of life.
Where others might have died in a ditch by the roadside, I survived.
I learned a very important adage on the road of life:
That "the truth shall set you free", and truer words were never spoken.
I used to build a fortress of lies upon lies,
But now, I am only armed with the words of truth.
And, the lies have all crumbled before me.
I don't have nearly as much as I used to,
and I realize that I never will again.
But, I'm happier now than I have ever been in my life.
So I guess that is really addition by subtraction.
Even though I'm not accepted as easily as I once was,
I'd rather be a majority of one
Than to be in the minority of millions.

I Am...

...staring death
Right in the face,
And neither one of us is blinking.
We have played this game for much too long.
It ends tonight.
No turning back for either of us.
We've squared off to each other, and
Both of us are as tense as can be.
This is the final showdown.
We scream like madmen at each other.
Like being shot from a cannon,
We spring at each other.
Bam!
What the....!
What happened?
What kind of trick is this?
He looks as surprised as I do.
What did we hit?
Doesn't matter.
We still stand our ground,
Not giving each other an inch.
This is my Domain!
Mine, I tell you!
No more
Of this cat and mousing around.
We have stalked each other,
Day after day,
For months on end.
I used to be the top dog around here,
Before he showed up.
I was respected,
And even feared.
Now,
There are too many cooks in the kitchen.
But it all ends tonight.
I refuse to cower like some cur.
I will not go silently into the night without a fight.
He'll have wounds aplenty to lick after I'm done with him tonight.
I will die fighting for what's rightfully mine.

Just the site of him, evokes some kind of unearthly growl,
From the nether pits of Hell within me.

Is that me?
Sounding like that?
I've never hated anyone so completely.
I can't seem to control myself.
I just turn into pure animalistic rage.
All I can see is red when we look at each other.
But, it all ends tonight, with this duel to the death.
There will be no tomorrow for one of us.
We stand ten paces apart as we square off against each other.
Both of us are as tense as could possibly be.
This is the final showdown.
I am the match and his Cheshire grin is the fuse.
It's now or never, with no turning back.
We both believe in Death before Dishonor.
We scream like madmen at each other.
Like being shot from a cannon,
We spring at each other.
Bam!
Again?
What just happened?
How is this so?
He looks as surprised as I do.
What did we hit?
Are the gods above and the demons below just playing with us?
My vengeance will not be abated.
Then I hear a voice from afar,
"It's just those stupid tom cats."
"They hit the bedroom window again,
One more time and I bet it'll break!"
"Scat cat!"
One day,
And one day soon,
He will get what's coming to him.
He'll be staring death
Right in the face.
That I can guarantee you.
Meow.
Purr.

I Am...

...terrified.
Silently,
You here the screams of
Whack... Whack... Whack...
It's just past the witching hour
On a midsummer's hottest night of the year.
The full moon is high overhead,
Casting its shadow over the living and the dead.
Everything is calm,
Like right before a storm.
Everyone should be asleep within my house.
I, myself, should have fallen asleep awhile ago.
But I haven't.
I hear things.
Like rolling thunder across the plains,
Whack... Whack... Whack...
The music from _Psycho_ plays in my mind.
I sense movement all around me.
I hear the pitter-patter of what I hope
Are my puppy dog's footsteps on the stairs.
I hear the rhythmic snoring of my wife.
Envying her slumber, I make sure we are all tucked in.
I hear my house creak and groan
As if some unnatural being is stalking about.
Whack... Whack... Whack...
My puppy dog yelps in his sleep.
I hope they didn't just get him.
All the while, I say a quick prayer
That I've locked my bedroom door.
If I haven't,
Well,
They could come inside
And do whatever to us.
Because if they come into your room,
And a leg or arm is not covered by your blanket,
Whack... Whack... Whack...
Off the limb goes.
All that's left is just a bloody stump.
Did I lock our door?
Did my wife forget to lock it when she got a drink of water?
The hardwood floor creaks right outside my room.
Oh God,

125

They're here!
I pull the covers over us,
Hoping I have covered us all up.
The smell of my sweat pushes past my nose,
And I hear an unearthly groan from the den.
Was that some creature from the yearning, nether depths,
Or a cat stepping on the remote control?
My wife throws the blankets aside with a sigh
As I lurch in horror to replace them.
I don't want her to lose an arm or a leg.
I hear the Whack, Whack, Whack echo of the axe
As it cleaves through my nightmares in crisp strokes.
I cover us from head to toe,
Making sure we will remain whole until morning.
I know these demons will be banished back to their realm
By Dawn's early light.
But Dawn is hours away,
And the natives are restless tonight.
Did you hear that?
It's right outside the door.
SSSHHHHH!!!
Whack... Whack... Whack...
Don't say a word.
Don't even think too loudly.
Keep your fingers and toes under the blanket
Or else they'll make a nice necklace
Around the neck of some demon, spawned in the fires of Hell.
This fight goes on every night.
My wife wonders why I'm so tired during the day?
It's because at night
I'm on guard,
Ever vigilant,
Making sure that my loved ones remain safe
And in one piece, throughout the night.
Whether it's real or just a nightmare,
Whack... Whack... Whack...
Continually echoes throughout my consciousness.

I Am...

...the Best.
I mean, someone has to be, right?
So why can't that someone be me?
Well it is.
I'm the best poet,
As this book definitely proves.
I'm the best Karate teacher,
Because, no other teacher has a resume as impressive as mine.
My karate students have won college scholarships,
And state championships in at least three states:
Alabama, Arkansas, & Kentucky.
We've won National and International tournaments
In Atlanta, Little Rock, Louisville, Memphis, and Washington DC.
I'm the best Husband,
Because I have the best wife.
I love you, Sabra.
I'm the best Father,
For the same reason as above.
My wife and children make me the best Father.
They make being great so easy.
Anyway, back to the subject at hand.
I have the best smile,
Thanks to the sacrifices my Mom and Dad made,
So that I could have braces.
I cook the best cheeseburgers.
I bet Jimmy Buffet would write another song,
"Cheeseburger in Paradise-II"
About my great cheeseburgers.
I'm the best Miami Dolphin fan,
And Baltimore Orioles fan there is.
I said fan,
Not fanatic.
There is a difference.
Is it hard being the best?
With a sly smile, I must say
That it comes pretty easily.
One must know his/her limitations.
You can't be the best at everything,
Or that would make you God.

And, since we already have a great God,
There's not much room for another.
I know, I'm not the best at fixing cars,
Or really at anything mechanical.
So, I stay far away from that situation.
I'm the best at stimulating the economy,
To get the job done when I have no bloody idea.
Anything that I participate in,
I go in with the attitude that I will be the best at it.
If I'm not the best at it,
I'll damn well pretend to be.
Why go about saying
"This is the 1,589th best cheeseburger you've ever had"?
No.
You say
"This is the best cheeseburger ever, that you're about to eat"!
Believe in yourself.
Because if you don't,
Then why should anyone else?
Be excited about yourself.
Others will catch your fever, as well.
And if you do end up cooking the 1,589th best cheeseburger
That they've ever eaten;
Take a step back,
And learn from your mistake(s).
Never stop believing that you can be the best.
No one can stop you from excelling.
Well,
There is one person who can,
And that one person is you.
So, stop being your own worst enemy.
Step out of your shadows
And show the world
All the things that you can do best.
They just won't be all the things that I'm best at!

I Am...

...the Holy Spirit.
Ten out of ten people will give you a different definition of me,
And most of them will be wrong.
Go ahead,
Ask the few people around you
What the Holy Spirit is.
I'm sure they'll come close to your definition,
Which is not exact.
That's where this poem comes into play.
This is going to give an exact understanding
Of what the Holy Spirit is all about.
The Holy Spirit is all of us, collectively.
When I say all of us,
I mean everyone who has ever lived,
And everyone who ever will live.
We are part of the Trinity.
It only makes sense, really.
Since God is a part of us,
This makes us a part of God.
When we die,
We go back into the Holy Spirit.
There is no Heaven, as in, fluffy clouds and streets of gold.
We go back to our Father,
And our Father is God.
Jesus taught us
That we would not recognize our loved ones when we die.
This is because the Holy Spirit is just one big melting pot.
Don't you get it?
Each of our souls are formed from this melting pot.
This is as close to reincarnation as it gets, because
We all get a sliver of each soul in the melting pot.
Everyone born after 1945 has a little piece of Hitler inside them
Just as we have a bit of Abraham Lincoln inside of us.
We have bits of English, Swedish, Arabic, and Mexican in all of us.
So when you hate a different culture;
You are really just hating yourself.

I Am...

...the hunger.
I am that which you crave.
I want you to be addicted to me in all ways.
I want to be the start of each day,
As well as, the end to every night;
Along with having me all throughout the day.
I want to be with you no matter where you go.
I'll be there, close to your heart.
Your senses are so attuned to me, that no matter where you go,
If I'm there, you'll know it almost immediately.
I can't wait to feel the soft caresses of your lips upon me.
I want to hear your intake of breath, which I know is so hot,
Quicken in anticipation of me.
I want you to breathe me in ever deeper and hold it,
As we become one.
Big Sigh
Why is it then, that others try to keep us apart?
Are they jealous?
They say I'm no good for you.
Some even say that I'll be the death of you.
I say they are the ones blowing smoke.
They say I'm just a lean, mean, killing machine,
And that to know me is to taste death.
I say we call their bluff.
Do they make you feel like I do?
No matter how they make you feel,
You always, always, come back to me.
Can these so-called friends comfort you, the way I can?
But we can prove them wrong, can't we?
Do you just toss me aside?
Or,
Do I kill you with the only kind of love and affection,
I know how to give?

I am...
... an ode to a cigarette.

I Am...

...the meaning of life.
Everyday, people around the world search and search for me,
And none of them realize that when they come into contact with me,
They are coming into contact with the meaning of life.
My motto is...
I am,
Therefore that is the meaning.
Sounds confusing?
It isn't really, when you think about it.
The saying goes,
That no man, be it male or female, is an island. Right?
Stay with me, here.
The meaning of life is to validate one's existence and
To give purpose to one's life.
We do that by interacting with each other.
No matter how casual that interaction is,
Once we have done so,
We have exercised the meaning of life.
We are giving purpose to our being,
By merely interacting with someone else.
And believe me,
Everybody interacts with someone else.
We are always reaching out to touch somebody,
No matter where we are in the world.
From outer space to the bottom of the deepest ocean,
We are in constant contact with someone.
Even a hermit comes into contact with someone at sometime.
As long as we are here, in this plane of reality,
Be it dead or alive,
We give purpose to another's life.
We are passing the meaning of life on to that someone,
All without them even being aware of what is happening.
So stop fretting over
Not being able to find the meaning to your life.
Surprise!
You have already found it!!
If it's not what you expected,
You should change who you come into contact with.

I Am...

...the Rod of Enlightenment.

'I will fear no evil, for you are with me;
Your rod and your staff, they comfort me,'
'The rod of correction imparts wisdom,
But a child left to himself, disgraces his mother.'

The word rod, has multiple meanings:
There are rods for the back of fools, rods of discipline,
There is even a rod of the wicked,
Along with a weaver's rod and The Rod of God.
All of these rods have different meanings.
But, as the Rod of Enlightenment,
I am not a physical object
That can be turned into a weapon
Against the weak and helpless or foolish.
I'm sure you have heard of me in various quotes.

"Spare the rod... and spoil the child",
Or "Thy rod and thy staff shall comfort me".

These words were written thousands of years ago.
They had a different meaning then.
These quotes have nothing to do with physical violence.
The rod in question is one of wisdom and intelligence,
Not of corporal punishment.
Spare the smarts and spoil the child, and in doing so,
Hinder the child from reaching their potential in adulthood.
Staff is another word for strength:
So when you read the quote,
'Thy rod and thy staff shall comfort me',
It should be read like this,
Thy wisdom and thy strength shall comfort me.
Reading the verse this way makes it as beautiful today
As I'm sure it was thousands of years ago.
What could be more secure than having
God's wisdom and strength to back you up?

I Am...

...waking up.
I'm a little disorientated.
Big yawn as I roll around to get comfortable.
I see we're still on the road.
How many hours have I been out?
It's dark now,
So at least two or three.
How much further do we have to go?
We seem to be out in the middle of nowhere,
Driving on some two-lane highway.
Not a ?&*#ing streetlight to be seen.
That must mean,
We're in Mississippi.
I see my darling husband is trying to kill us
With his Transporter-like driving skills.
I don't think he knows I'm awake.
Are we going to pass this car,
Or are we just going to keep tailgating it?
God,
We are so close.
Is he trying to scare me?
I know we had an argument,
But is he trying to kill us?
No,
Not us,
He'd never harm the babies,
But me.
Is he trying to kill me?
I see lights coming from up ahead,
He needs to pass this guy
And get over.
Any time now
Would be nice.
He's not getting over,
And the lights are getting brighter and closer.
Does he want to kill the babies,
As well as me?
Does he hate me that much?
He said such cruel things to me.
I wish he had hit me instead.

Why won't he pass this guy?
Does he want to see me squirm?
I won't give him the satisfaction.
Why did I ever marry him?
I know he wants the insurance money,
I just know it.
I thought he canceled that policy on me.
I guess,
He is trying to cancel me now.
Why is he passing on a curve,
With a car coming at us?
Doesn't that other car see us?
Why isn't he getting out of the way?
Should I jerk the wheel?
Damn.
That oncoming car is getting closer and closer.
Pass the car or just back off and get over.
Should I say something?
Should I yell something?
Did I wake up,
Just a couple of minutes ago,
To be awake for my death?
Oh my God,
The babies!
The other car seems to be coming straight for us.
He's not getting over!
It's like we are playing some insane game of chicken.
We ARE going to die!
I jerk,
I yell,
I scream,
As the car passes harmlessly by us,
On a divided highway.
I hear my husband laughing at me.
The bastard!

I Am...

...wanting.
Wanting to stir your heart,
Your passions,
Your fervor,
Your hearts desires:
All in that first kiss
Last Kiss,
Every Kiss,
That we share.
I want to cascade
Kisses over your body,
And capture your soul,
Like the ocean's waves
Endless onslaught on the shore.
I want to quench
The raging fires within you,
Like a monsoon does an African jungle.
I want to be the sun source everyday of your life,
Warming your skin,
Your heart and your very soul.
Banishing forever the darkest recesses
Of your soul before my light.
I want to be the end-all of every desire
You have ever fantasized about.
I want to be the love that you have longed for so much.
Are you believing what you are reading?
Do you sense my passion,
My desire for you, on this page?
No matter how far away,
Or how close, we might really be,
I am right here, right now.
Find me, feel me, love me like never before.
As long as you remember that which you have read,

You will always have me with you.

XOXO
Kelly Klemetsrud

I Am...

...wanting (as usual),
To be appreciated.
Isn't that what everybody wants?
Some might disagree and say they want love,
But love is easy to be found.
I mean, look around you and see how many people are in love.
You see them kissing, hugging, holding hands,
Or even yelling and screaming at each other.
But how many of these "in love" people feel appreciated?
What is the one thing people want more than anything?
Love? Acceptance? Respect? Fame? Money?
Love is desired.
Acceptance is wanted.
Respect is either given, deserved, or earned.
Fame is always fleeting.
And money is the root of all things evil.
Whereas appreciation is valued by everyone.
I've known people who don't believe in love.
But show me someone who does not want to be appreciated,
And I'll show you a cynic.
Do you know what a cynic is?
A cynic is someone who knows the price of everything,
But the value of nothing.
Just make sure to give as much appreciation as you want to receive,
Because appreciation is like a Christmas gift;
It's better to give than to receive.
Believe me when I say,
The more you give, the more you'll receive.

I Am...

...your destiny.
At least until the end of this poem.
Dwell on this thought for a moment.
You have lived your entire life,
To the very nanosecond,
To be able to read this poem.
So is that predestination?
Were you destined at the dawn of time to read these words?
God does know the future, or so we are taught.
But we are taught wrong, in a sense.
Every time we make, or don't make, a choice,
God is aware of the outcome of said choice.
It could be the most mundane of choices:
Say having an extra cup of coffee one morning,
Which gives you a caffeine buzz.
Causing you to push the wrong button, by mistake,
And crash a computer system at work.
Thus, resulting in a termination of employment.
Not likely, I'm sure, in this world.
But there is an alternative world
Where that does happen to you.
God knows the ramifications of each choice,
Or non-choice.
So you see,
God doesn't just know the future,
God knows every future,
That will (or will not) happen in our reality.
So nothing is predestined.
Because if it was,
That would mean
We don't have a choice in said matter.
And we always have a choice.
No one in the history of humankind
Was predestined to do anything.
How about the King of England
Abdicating his throne
To marry a commoner,
An American, to say the least.
King Edward VIII was destined
To be the second most powerful man in the world,
Behind the President of the United States.
But he gave it all up for love.

He changed his destiny
Even though he was predestined to become King,
And to stay King, until death.
We are never predestined to do anything.
Not even Jesus was predestined to be the Christ.
I know this will rankle some fur,
But read with an open mind,
And this will all make sense.
Jesus simply chose to be the Christ,
Just as we could choose to do the same.
But we choose not to.
Jesus was just as human as you and I.
He was not Superman in a spandex robe.
There was nothing that Jesus did
That you or I could not do.
That's what makes Jesus so cool.
He had the same wants and desires
That every human has.
But he ignored his wants and simply
Chose to keep doing the right thing(s).
And by doing so, the title Christ was bestowed upon him.
A title which he chose to accept.
Jesus could have stopped being the Christ
Anytime he wanted to.
If he didn't have the choice of being the Christ,
It all would have been for nothing.
Jesus would have just been a puppet,
Doing the bidding of some god-like Geppetto.
Jesus chose to sacrifice for us all:
God never forced Jesus to make his choice.
Jesus did so of his own accord.
It all comes down to making a choice:
Be it a good one,
Bad one,
The right choice,
Or the wrong choice.
We all have a choice to make,
Or, not to make.
That my friend...
Is your true destiny.

I Am...

...your kiss.
I see the flirting,
And all the hopes and desires that are connected with said flirtations.
But most importantly,
I see your want.
I see how you lick your lips and smile.
A smile so genuine, so real
That it almost masks all your fears and inhibitions.
I know you are scared:
Scared that he's not having the same feelings as you,
Scared that you are the only one wanting what you want.
I see as both heads dip and turn.
I see the lips part in anticipation.
You pull back,
Not wanting to send the wrong signals.
But your smiles keep him entranced.
You might not be on the dance floor,
But you are dancing.
And he seems to be dancing with you, as well.
He touches your hand:
Was that a spark that passed between you?
Like the song says, "It's now or never".
You caress his cheek with the back of your fingers,
As you lean closer.
At first, you just brush his lips with yours.
The second kiss lasts just a second, which is just way too short.
You nuzzle his face with back of your hand,
Trace around his neck to hold him tighter
So you can breathe him in, and then you kiss him.
Your lips meet as your tongues just barely touch.
What a beautiful sight to see!
You kiss him so passionately, so honestly.
How can something be so wanton yet so innocent at the same time?
Wow!
Honestly, I'm not your kiss:
I just wish your kiss was mine.

I Am...

...your passions,
Your lusts,
Your Zeal,
All pitched to a frenzied climax
That comes together
In our first kiss,
Our last kiss,
And every kiss in-between,
As we mold our souls,
From the singular to the plural,
As two lost souls find one another
To become a single entity.
I want to grab you and hold onto you,
While we make love to each other,
As furiously as
The Surf's endless onslaught upon the shore,
But as gentle as
A midsummer's night breeze,
that refreshes everything it caresses.
I want to quench the fires inside of you,
As easily as
Niagara drowns the rocks beneath it.
I want to be your sun-source,
As you are mine,
Warming your skin,
Your heart, your very soul.
All the while, banishing your darkest and deepest fears,
Before my light.
I want to be that lover which you feared you would never find.
I want to be the answer to all those prayers that
You cried to God through those endless lonely nights.
Because
That is exactly what you are to me,
and much, much, more.

Afterthought

All good things come to an end... bad things, too. If you ever find yourself in a situation that is not healthy to you, either mentally, physically, or spiritually, please get help. Please do not protect the bad guy or gal. You deserve a better life. Stop punishing yourself for something that should have been either forgotten or forgiven. Life goes on... whether we are in it or not. Be a part of life again and take the steps to get help.

Thank you for reading the 101 best poems ever written: I mean, that I have ever written. No matter how truthful or authentic these poems might have sounded, or how they reminded you of someone you might know or I might know, all these poems are works of fiction. They are based on reality, but they aren't based on my reality, or any of my family's reality. I talk to a lot of people and I pick up a snippet here and a snippet there, and tie them all together into a great poem. I make the subject into a personal situation so people can connect to the poem. Any mention of lovers or ex-lovers, or ex-wives or any member of my wife's or ex-wife's family were just inserted to make the poems more realistic.

My next book will be entitled, "Perceptions of a Father". It will have a picture of my father on the cover.

Please feel free to leave comments at myultimatetruths@aol.com

Smiles,

Kelly Klemetsrud

FEAR THE 'FINS..!!